The
Berlin
S-Bahn

BRIAN HARDY

Capital Transport

Author's Note

This book is designed to give an appreciation and understanding of the S-Bahn (Schnellbahn – rapid transit railway) system in Berlin, outlining its history, development, setbacks and subsequent renaissance. The political problems, difficulties and divisions which existed for over four decades have all added to tell a remarkable story – it is hoped that this work gives readers a fair and balanced account, along with providing useful facts and figures. For more detailed research, however, readers must read German, for there are many fine publications about both the U-Bahn and S-Bahn systems, with often one complete book being devoted to a particular subject. Readers interested in track layouts are recommended to consult the excellent track maps of Berlin by Quail.

No work of this kind is ever the result of one person's efforts and thanks are due to Jeanne Hardy for her help and support in the preparation of the book, along with Nick Agnew, Alan Blake, Bob Greenaway, John Laker, Brian Patton and Steve Williams in responding to my request for photographs – the final selection has been a formidable but enjoyable task.

Your writer is most grateful to the S-Bahn Berlin Transport Authority (S-Bahn GmbH), Peter Bley and members of the S-Bahn preservation group in Berlin, and to Bert Steinkamp (from Holland).

But the greatest appreciation of all must go jointly to Dr Volker Wangemann of Berlin and Brian Patton here in Great Britain, both of whom checked the text for accuracy and researched and supplied the answers to what must have seemed a never-ending barrage of questions.

Ickenham, Middlesex, March 1996　　　　BRIAN HARDY

ISBN 185414 185 6

Published by Capital Transport Publishing
38 Long Elmes, Harrow Weald, Middlesex

Printed by CS Graphics, Singapore

Contents

Front cover An eight-car class 477 train approaches Karlshorst on a daytime short working of S3 from Erkner to Hauptbahnhof. *Brian Hardy*

Back cover Rear of a rebuilt 476 stock train at Lichtenberg, the main Berlin railway station of former East Germany, served by three S-Bahn lines. *Capital Transport*

Berlin – The Historical Background

Readers must appreciate that the following notes are but a very brief summary of what is an extremely complicated history of the City of Berlin.

The first recorded mention of Berlin was made in 1237, the year usually taken as that of the City's foundation, though it is probable that people had lived in the site before then. It was a small trading post situated on the northern bank of the River Spree, in the area now known as the Nikolaiviertel (Nikolai Quarter) just to the south of the present city hall. Opposite, on what is now the Museum Island, was a settlement of fisherfolk, known as Cölln. Gradually, the two communities grew together and expanded. By the beginning of the railway age, Berlin had become the capital of the Kingdom of Prussia. Around it were separate towns such as Charlottenburg and Cöpenick (Köpenick).

The foundation of the German Empire in January 1871 gave a great impetus to the growth of Berlin, whose population grew from 826,000 in 1871 to almost four million by 1914. The change from kingdom to empire did not directly affect either the railways or the internal transport of the city, since both remained matters for the government of Prussia and the local authorities, but of course the growth in population did call for improved public transport. Administratively, there was for many years no change and Berlin remained little more than the present borough of Mitte (Middle). Only in the early part of this century was it appreciated that a more unified structure was required to tackle the problems of the city's utilities and in 1911 an Act of the Prussian Parliament created the Zweckverband Gross-Berlin (something akin to the Metropolitan Board of Works in nineteenth-century London), one of the tasks of which was to be the co-ordination of public transport. However, not much had been achieved when war broke out in 1914. In 1919 the main tramway company, Grosse Berliner Strassenbahn AG, sold its undertaking to the Zweckverband.

The new government which replaced the empire decided to tackle the question afresh and in 1920 passed the Gross-Berlin Gesetz (Greater Berlin Act), setting up a new municipality to cover the entire area of greater Berlin, though the 20 individual boroughs still retained many powers in matters other than transport.

After the collapse of Berlin in 1945, the city was divided into sectors – it had been intended that there would be three, but when the French claimed a share, a sector was created for them from those of the other western allies. The pre-war boroughs were therefore divided among four powers, the Russians taking eight, situated in the eastern part of the city, the former power-base of the Communist Party. As the borough boundaries were no more logical than those in London, anomalies were created, and Potsdamer Platz, for example, parts of which were in Kreuzberg, Mitte and Tiergarten, now found itself in three sectors!

These considerations did not matter too much in the early post-war years, but as the Russians and the western allies began to drift apart, the consequences became more serious. Each side had set up a municipal administration in its area and by 1949 this led to the splitting of transport between a BVG (West) and a BVG (East). Gradually, the western sectors grew together while they became more and more cut off from the hinterland of Berlin. From June 1952, for example, free access to the territory of what was then the DDR was no longer allowed to inhabitants of West Berlin. The culmination of this process was, of course, the night of 12/13 August 1961, with what is generally known as the building of the Berlin Wall, but what, in DDR-speak, was known as the securing of the frontier. A few weeks later, it became very difficult for West Berliners to visit the eastern part of the city and almost impossible for the residents there to come to the west. This remained the case for some time, though the restriction on West Berliners and on senior citizens from the east were gradually eased, particularly after the development of the 'Ostpolitik' by Willy Brandt in the early-1970s and the replacement of Walter Ulbricht as DDR leader by Erich Honecker. On 3 September 1971 an agreement, to take effect from 3 June 1972, guaranteed access and visiting rights for West Berliners to the eastern part of the city.

After the building of the Wall, the eastern part of the city was briefly known as 'Democratic Berlin', thereafter as 'Hauptstadt der DDR, Berlin' ('Capital City of the DDR, Berlin'). 'East Berlin', a term widely used by westerners, had no official meaning. Depending on one's point of view, the remainder of the City was Berlin (West), West Berlin, or 'the special political enclave known as West Berlin'. This part of the city became a Land of the Federal Republic, a Senate replacing the former Magistrate (City Council). Much of its economic life was heavily subsidised, but despite that, with an ageing population, it began to show signs of decline and it was difficult to attract labour to Berlin.

All references to the west and its transport facilities were deleted from maps in the east, where it had become a non-place, but the reverse was not the case. In practice, contact between the two parts increased over the years – sometimes, as in the events to mark the 750th anniversary, competition took the place of confrontation.

All this came to an abrupt (and surprising) end with the reopening of the frontier on the night of 9 November 1989. Immediately afterwards co-operation between the two civic administrations began and considerable progress was made, even before formal reunification took place. In 1991 it was agreed that Berlin should in due course become the Land of Berlin/Brandenburg. Government is still in Bonn at the time of writing (1996) but is to move back to Berlin. Much work is now under way to translate this decision into bricks and mortar, concrete and glass, by the end of the century.

The Development of the S-Bahn

In the first half of the 19th century, the built-up area of Berlin comprised little more than the centre of the eastern part of the present city. The western part formed the separate town of Charlottenburg, while the various suburban communities were villages in the surrounding countryside. Berlin was still a fortified city, surrounded by walls, access through which was by gates. Of these, the most famous was, and still is, the Brandenburger Tor.

The Radial Network
The railway age in the area began on 22 September 1838, with the opening of the line from the village of Zehlendorf to Potsdam. This was extended inwards to a terminus at the Potsdamer Bahnhof on 29 October of the same year. On 1 July 1841 the Berlin-Anhalt Railway opened from Berlin as far as Jüterbog, although Dessau – Köthen had previously opened on 1 September 1840. In the following year, two further lines were brought into service – the Berlin–Stettin Railway began operation on the line to Eberswalde via Bernau (1 August) and the Berlin-Frankfurt Railway began passenger services to Frankfurt (Oder) via Cöpenick on 23 October.

There was then a gap of a few years until the Berlin–Hamburg Railway opened its line from Berlin to Boitzenburg via Spandau on 15 October 1846. Its terminus, the Hamburger Bahnhof in Invalidenstrasse, is the only original station in Berlin to survive, though it is now used as a museum. The other companies also erected termini, all but the Frankfurter Bahnhof being located just outside the walls of the city. These in most cases were replaced in the 1870s and 1880s by new and more spacious premises, some

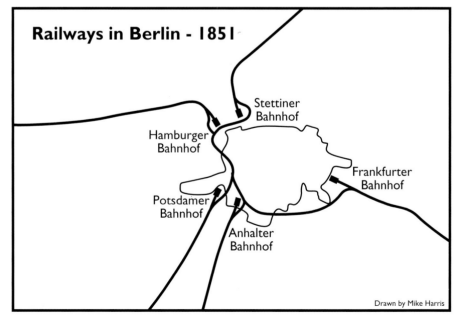

Railways in Berlin - 1851

Stettiner Bahnhof

Hamburger Bahnhof

Frankfurter Bahnhof

Potsdamer Bahnhof

Anhalter Bahnhof

Drawn by Mike Harris

of very considerable architectural merit. Of these, only the Schlesischer Bahnhof, now renamed Berlin Hauptbahnhof, survives although not in its original form. The others had all fallen out of use by 1952, since the access lines were located in what were by then the sectors administered by the western allies, while the lines which they served all passed through the new DDR. At a period when most Berliners wanted to sever links with the past, there were few protests when the stations were successively demolished. Many now regret this.

The revolution of 1848, which considerably frightened the government of Prussia, also highlighted the inconvenience of the separate termini and it was decided to build a connecting line. This was opened on 15 October 1851 in the form of a half-circle running, mainly in the streets, from the Stettiner to the Frankfurter Bahnhof. Other than military trains, it did not carry a passenger service but it had a considerable value for freight operation. However, it interfered with road traffic and from 1864 was used only at night.

On 13 September 1866, the Berlin–Görlitz Railway opened its line to Cottbus via Grünau and Königs Wusterhausen, followed by the Ostbahn between Ostbahnhof and Küstrin via Mahlsdorf on 1 October 1867. By 1879 therefore, Berlin, which had meanwhile become the capital of the new German Empire, was linked by rail with every important city in the country and the foundation of what was subsequently to become the S-Bahn had been laid. Gaps in the network were closed by new construction over the next few decades. The 'old' Wannseebahn, from Zehlendorf to Wannsee and Neubabelsberg was opened for passenger traffic on 1 June 1874, providing a useful relief to the Potsdam line. In 1875 the Berlin–Dresden line via Mahlow and Zossen was brought into operation on 17 June and two years later on 10 July 1877, the Northern Railway opened its line from Gesundbrunnen to Neubrandenburg via Oranienburg, and this was linked to the Stettiner Bahnhof on 1 December of the same year. Passenger services on the Wetzlarer Bahn from Grunewald to Blankenheim via Wannsee began on 15 April 1879. Finally, two further lines, of local importance, were opened – from Schönholz to Velten on 1 October 1893 and from Lichtenberg to Werneuchen via Ahrensfelde on 1 May 1898. The radial network was now complete.

All the lines mentioned above had been operated by private companies and, as in Great Britain but unlike practice in France, the railway network was not built following any definite plan. Nationalisation began early in Prussia, with the takeover of the Niederschlesisch-Märkische Railway in 1852 but most companies retained their independence until the 1880s, when they were successively absorbed into the Königliche Preussische Eisenbahn Verwaltung (Royal Prussian Railway Administration). With the nationalisation of the Berlin–Dresden Railway on 1 May 1887, the process was complete. The impetus for this was military rather than economic or social and it came too late to have any real effect on planning. Other states of the German Empire retained their own railways until 1 April 1920, when almost all of these were amalgamated into the Deutsche Reichsbahn-Gesellschaft (German State Railway Company), normally referred to as DRG.

It should be noted that the above summary of what is a very complicated history is intended to simplify matters for readers who are not too familiar with the political or economic history of Berlin and Germany. The story of the terminal stations in particular is complex, since many of these were rebuilt and there were, for example, two stations bearing the name of Anhalter Bahnhof. It should also be noted that the names of some of the original lines are still used to denote particular lines of the network – the line to Tegel, for example, is often referred to in railway parlance as the Kremmener Bahn.

Berlin also became one of the main centres of the railway industry in Germany and locomotive builders such as Borsig established large works in the then outer area. Around these sprang up industrial suburbs with densely-packed working-class housing.

The Ring

By the 1860s, the original connecting line was totally inadequate for the goods traffic now on offer and in 1867 it was decided to build a new connecting line, rather further out from the centre, to cater for both passenger and goods traffic. The first portion of this Neue Verbindungsbahn (New Connecting Railway) was opened for goods traffic between Moabit, Stralau (now Ostkreuz) and Schöneberg on 17 July 1871, passenger traffic following on 1 January the following year. The old connecting line was then closed, except for a short portion which served a gasworks. On 15 November 1877, the Ring was completed by a line from Moabit to Schöneberg via Charlottenburg (now Westend). Trains ran to and from the various termini or had connections with these and to accommodate this traffic at the Potsdamer Bahnhof, a separate station, Potsdamer Ringbahnhof, was added at the eastern side of the main line terminus in 1891.

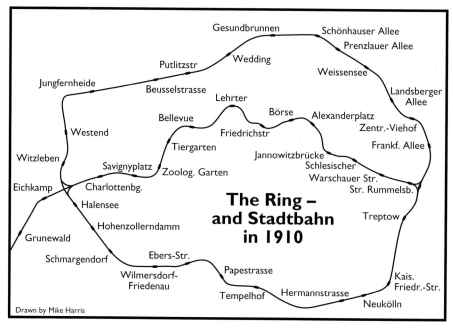

The Ring – and Stadtbahn in 1910

Drawn by Mike Harris

The Stadtbahn

In 1871 an architect, August Orth, published a plan for connecting lines across the centre of Berlin. These plans envisaged an east-west link on viaduct and a north-south line in tunnel. Apart from relieving the various termini, these lines would also encourage the inhabitants to move out into the suburbs. The idea of the north-south tunnel proved to be beyond contemporary technology but in 1872 the Deutsche Eisenbahn-Baugesell-schaft (German Railway Construction Company) was formed to build the line from Charlottenburg in the west to the Schlesischer Bahnhof in the east, with a further link to the south-west. Even at that date, the density of building in central Berlin made it difficult to find a route. The first preference was for a line running to the south of the present line and rather shorter than it, but this foundered on the grounds of cost. The next plan provided for the use of the Royal Canal, which was to be closed, from the east to Friedrichstrasse and this was the route that was in fact used, though the government dithered for a while about the actual closure of the waterway. West of

Friedrichstrasse the crossing of the open space of the Tiergarten caused problems, as the government would not have a railway slicing right across this attractive park and a tunnel would have involved ramps beyond the capacity of contemporary locomotives. The next plan was rejected by the military.

It was not until May 1878 that agreement was finally reached, for a line along the present route and construction began in the following year. But by then there were financial problems and, after the failure of the company, which had in 1874 been reconstructed, with some state capital, as the Berliner Stadt-Eisenbahn-Gesellschaft, the line was completed by the Prussian state. The engineer was Ernst Dircksen, who had also been responsible for the construction of the Ring. Known ever since simply as the Stadtbahn, the line, which runs mainly on viaduct, was opened by Kaiser Wilhelm I on 7 February 1882. At first it was used by local traffic only. The southern pair of lines, to be used by long-distance trains, were brought into service on 15 May 1882. Two months later, all east-west local traffic was diverted onto the new lines. Connecting curves at various places linked it to radial lines.

The foundation of the Empire gave a great impetus to the growth of Berlin, whose population increased from 400,000 in 1845 to almost two million in 1900, by which date a further 750,000 lived in the suburban area. While many of the people who flocked into the city found homes in the tenement blocks known as Mietskasernen (Rent Barracks), some began to settle in the suburbs. The Ring and Stadtbahn passed through areas which were already built up and so had from the beginning the functions of a metropolitan railway. Growth of railway-based suburbs came rather later and may be taken to date from 1868, when a station was opened at Lichterfelde on the Anhalter Bahn. This was a constructed by a builder named Carstenn, who was developing a Villenkolonie (middle-class housing) in the area and required a connection with Berlin. Not only did he have to build the station and connecting lines, but he also had to guarantee the Company a yearly subsidy of 600 Gulden. In return, the railway provided three services each way per day, by main line trains. In the same year, the Berlin-Hamburg Company began to run workmen's trains to Spandau for workers in the ordnance factory. The government insisted on the provision of cheap fares and provided a subsidy for this.

Gradually, other companies began to see that money could be made from suburban traffic and in particular from developers and thus many new stations were opened on the model of Lichterfelde after 1880. Soon, problems of overcrowding and congestion began to be experienced and on 1 October 1891 a new line was opened from the Wannseebahnhof, adjacent to the Potsdamer Bahnhof, to Zehlendorf, to connect with the 'old' Wannseebahn and allow a faster service to be given to the affluent south-western suburbs. Other suburban lines were doubled, as to Oranienburg in June 1892, or quadrupled, to allow the suburban traffic to operate independently of main line goods and passenger trains.

The growth of the suburban network was also helped by the adoption of a special tariff. The first special fare system for the Stadt- and Ringbahn, based on distance, was adopted in 1886, but in 1890 this was replaced by a zone system, itself further simplified in 1891. On 1 October of that year, a suburban tariff was instituted on all radial lines. The limits of this tariff – Oranienburg, Bernau, Strausberg, Königs Wusterhausen, Zossen, Werder and Nauen, basically defined what has been ever since been regarded as the suburban network. The name 'S-Bahn' was not used at this time, the lines being referred to as the Stadt-, Ring und Vorortbahnen der Königlich Preussische Eisenbahn Verwaltung (KPEV) – City, Ring and Suburban Railways of the Royal Prussian Railway Administration.

Electrification

It is perhaps surprising that although Berlin was the centre of the earliest experiments in electric traction, the city had to wait so long for the electrification of its suburban network. Given the political and economic difficulties with which operators had to contend, it is equally surprising that electrification ever happened at all.

The first proposal for electrification was made in 1899 by the Union-Elektrizitäts-Gesellschaft, later part of the AEG. This would have utilised third-rail collection at 600V d.c. Due to the estimated high cost of 43-million Mark (roughly £4.3-million), the project was abandoned. However, the managers of the KPEV were interested in the possibilities of electric traction and in 1898 they agreed to a proposal from Siemens and Halske for a trial operation on the Wannseebahn. A ten-car train entered service on 13 July 1900 (other sources give the date as 1 August) and remained in operation until 1 July 1902. The train was made up of nine three-axle coaches and one two-axle coach of compartment stock, of which the two end three-axle coaches were motored and the current was collected at 750V d.c. from a third rail. As the train had to run in service with steam trains, and to their timetable, a true evaluation of the benefits of electric traction could not be obtained from such a limited trial.

To gain wider experience, the KPEV then agreed to the electrification of the recently-opened line from Potsdamer Ringbahnhof to Gross-Lichterfelde-Ost and the first train ran on 4 June 1903. Again, current was supplied from a third rail, but at 550V d.c. and again compartment stock was used. There were 30 motor coaches, each having two 125 h.p. motors and these attained a speed of 50 km/hour. Full electric service began on 15 July 1903. This scheme was executed by UEG, who owned the trains and fixed installations until 1912, when these passed into the ownership of the KPEV. The service gave every satisfaction and the stock continued to operate until 2 July 1929, when the line was converted to become standard with the remainder of the S-Bahn.

The short branch from Schöneweide to Spindlersfeld was electrified at 6,000V, 25Hz a.c. on 15 August 1903. Trial running to test the feasibility of this form of electrification for main line rather than suburban operation was undertaken for almost a year without passengers and, when the tests proved successful, passenger trains began running on 4 July 1904. Motive power was two bogie motor coaches, which could pull up to three trailers and trains ran generally on an hourly headway. The line, however, at only 4 km, was really too short to simulate 'main line' conditions and electric operation came to an end on 1 March 1906. Further trials in the Hamburg area were also successful and it was decided to standardise on this form of electrification, but at 16.75 Hz, for main lines in Germany (and, later, also the Austro-Hungarian Empire and Switzerland).

Further proposals by UEG in 1903/04 and by Siemens and Halske in 1907 were not adopted, but the officials in the Ministry of Public Works had become convinced that the operation of steam trains in Berlin could not be continued indefinitely, particularly in view of the spectacular growth of traffic from 103-million passengers in 1897 to 165-million in 1906. The KPEV was not persuaded of the desirability of electrification, particularly in view of the cost, partly because with the T12 and T14 tank locomotives, it had developed motive power which could provide the same level of service as electric traction. The inhabitants of the inner districts had long complained of the noise and dirt associated with steam trains and as the service developed, so their grumbling increased. By 1900 there were 721 trains traversing the Stadtbahn daily and by 1913 there were 946. It was estimated that 70 tonnes of soot produced by steam engines descended on Berlin in a typical year. The KPEV therefore produced in 1909 concrete plans for electrification of the suburban network and in 1913 these plans were agreed by an Act of the Prussian parliament. The system proposed was to use current at 10kV a.c., 15Hz, with overhead current collection. Motive power was to be provided by small two-axle, non-driving locomotives placed at the head of the train, the driving position and current collection being in the leading coach. This would allow the continued use of existing compartment stock, although some professionals doubted the wisdom of this. Despite these reservations, and with an alteration to 15kV 16.75 Hz, trials began on the electrified line from Dessau to Bitterfeld in the summer of 1914 and some prototype trains were ordered. The outbreak of war put an end to the trials and delayed the delivery of the trains, which finally appeared in 1920, when they were placed in service on the line from Breslau to Görlitz. War similarly prevented another proposed trial, on the 4 km branch from Wannsee to Stahnsdorf Cemetery, of a system of third-rail operation at 1,600V d.c., with trains consisting of two bogie motor coaches flanking three four-wheel trailers.

Incredibly, only a month after the end of the fighting, the Minister of Public Works ordered the railways to begin planning for the electrification of the lines from the Stettiner Bahnhof to Bernau and Hermsdorf. Electrification of these 32.75 km would cost only a fraction of the sum needed for the entire network but would nevertheless yield significant improvements in service. The system to be adopted was to be 15kV a.c. at 16.66 Hz and compartment stock was to be used. Credits of 11-million Mark were voted in 1920 and the first masts were erected. In view of the growing financial crisis, however, these decisions were reversed in 1921 and instead a system of 800V d.c. third rail was substituted. Despite raging inflation, which led to the collapse of the currency at the end of 1923, work was pushed ahead steadily and on 8 August 1924, by which time monetary stability had been restored in the form of the Rentenmark, the first electric train ran from the Stettiner Vorortbahnhof (Stettiner suburban station) to Bernau. This date is normally regarded as the beginning of the present S-Bahn system. It was a triumph of determination over almost incredible difficulties. A full electric service on this line with an improved timetable, plus the electrification to Birkenwerder, was instituted on 5 June 1925. Electrification from Birkenwerder reached Oranienburg on 4 October of the same year.

Electrification of the northern lines was completed by the opening of service on the Kremmener Bahn from Schönholz to Velten on 16 March 1927. This particular section had been somewhat delayed as some of the track had to be doubled. The total length of electrified route was 70.5 km and the cost had been 13-million Mark.

The Great Electrification
Even before the electrification of the northern lines had been completed, the Board of DRG had decided, in July 1926, to electrify the Stadt- and Ringbahn and the associated lines to Spandau, Potsdam, Stahnsdorf, Kaulsdorf, Grünau, Erkner and Spindlersfeld. It was clear that steam traction no longer met passengers' expectations and there had been a relative loss of traffic to other forms of transport. Much of the locomotive-hauled compartment stock was by now life-expired, due to overwork and lack of maintenance during the war and the period of inflation. The new system was to have new signalling, to permit trains to operate on a headway of 90 seconds, new overhaul works and stabling facilities in Tempelhof and Erkner, a new power station and new trains. In this last aspect, DRG had clearly taken a different course from that adopted by the Southern Electric in the UK and from that originally envisaged by KPEV. The wisdom of building new trains instead of making do with adapted compartment stock has been amply justified by the long years of service rendered by the stock, sometimes under the most arduous conditions, during which the basic design has still not become outdated. There was also provision for a new connection between the Stadtbahn and the line to Spandau West and a station at the western intersection of the Stadt- and Ringbahn. Opened as Ausstellung (Exhibition), this became Westkreuz in 1932.

Work began in the late-summer of 1926 and the first trains were ordered in the autumn. Just under two years later, on 11 June 1928, the first electric trains went into service between Potsdam and Erkner via the Stadtbahn. Other sections were converted at frequent intervals and the last suburban steam train traversed the Stadtbahn on 20 March 1929, while full electric operation of the Ringbahn followed on 15 May the same year. Not for the last time had those charged with the operation of the Berlin suburban lines demonstrated a capacity for quick action! The capabilities of the new trains allowed considerable acceleration of services – the journey time from Friedrichstrasse to Erkner, for example, was reduced from 62 to 46 minutes. At peak periods, 28 trains per hour passed over the Stadtbahn in each direction.

The electrification dates for the other sections were as follows:

10 July 1928	Wannsee–Stahnsdorf
23 August 1928	Westkreuz–Spandau West
6 November 1928	Charlottenburg–Halensee and southern section of the Ringbahn to Neukölln, Treptower Park and Grünau
6 November 1928	Hauptbahnhof (then Schlesischer Bahnhof)–Kaulsdorf
1 February 1929	Schöneweide–Spindlersfeld
1 February 1929	Charlottenburg–Baumschulenweg (the northern section of the Ringbahn)
18 April 1929	Potsdamer Ringbahnhof–Papestrasse
18 April 1929	Halensee–Westend

The total length of electrified route was by now 229.48 km and the cost of recent project had been 159.8-million RM. The work was rounded off by the conversion of the line to Lichterfelde Ost from 550V to 800V, the replacement of the old rolling stock and by two short extensions – from Jungfernheide to Gartenfeld on 18 December 1929 and from Kaulsdorf to Mahlsdorf on 15 December 1930.

To mark the transformation, the network was officially renamed the S-Bahn (Schnellbahn [Rapid Transit]) on 1 December 1930, when the symbol of a white 'S' on a green disc was also adopted to denote third-rail electric lines – it has not been used on lines which remained steam-operated or have more recently been operated by diesel or overhead electric trains. The 'S' symbol soon became as well known and recognised as London's blue bar and red circle signs on the Underground. The Berliners took the new system and its symbol to their hearts, where both have remained almost ever since. The success of the scheme was soon demonstrated in increasing traffic figures, despite the onset of the great depression in 1930 and some increase in fares associated with that. The S-Bahn symbol is a general phenomenon all over Germany now, in those days Hamburg was the only other S-Bahn city.

The next candidate for electrification was the Wannseebahn, still served by steam trains which had now begun to look decidedly antiquated when compared with the new electrics serving other Berlin suburbs. Despite the economic crisis, work began in 1931 and electric service started on 15 May 1933. Apart from the electrification of the line itself, the parallel tracks of the main line were also energised between Potsdamer Bahnhof and Zehlendorf Mitte and the station at Schöneberg was rebuilt and relocated. New stations were built at Sundgauer Strasse and Feuerbachstrasse. The reason for the electrification of the main line was to allow the operation of the 'Bankierzüge' (Bankers' express trains) which ran non-stop to Zehlendorf to provide a fast service to the affluent suburbs of south-west Berlin. A scheduled speed of 70 km/hour over this stretch made the line the fastest inner suburban service then operating in Europe. With this electrification, the system was for the time being complete, and extensions would have to wait for the development of the outer suburbs.

The North-South Tunnel

Whilst the Stadtbahn had solved the problem of cross-city east-west traffic, Berlin continued to suffer from the disadvantage that the line serving the northern and southern suburbs still terminated at stations on the edge of the central area, the Stettiner Bahnhof and Potsdamer Bahnhof respectively. Plans to close this gap were first published as far back as 1910 and, given the built-up nature of the city, these were for a line in tunnel. Finally in 1933, the Board of DRG decided to build a line in tunnel from just north of the Stettiner Bahnhof to south of the Anhalter Bahnhof, thus allowing through operation of the suburban lines and affording relief to the Stettiner Bahnhof, the busiest of the city's termini.

The idea had pre-dated the formation of the Nazi government, but to the latter, with its sights fixed on the staging of the Olympic Games in Berlin in 1936, the building of the line afforded excellent opportunities for propaganda. Despite a tragic accident near the Brandenburger Tor on 20 August 1935, when a retaining wall fell into the tunnel killing 19 workmen, the line was completed from the northern portal to Unter den Linden and opened for passengers on 28 July 1936, just before the start of the Olympic Games. Further extension southwards was bedevilled by several changes of plan. In 1934 the idea of linking the new tunnel to the southern part of the Ring was developed, necessitating the redesign of the station at Potsdamer Platz from a simple island type to a four-road layout with two island platforms and, to the west, a flying junction with the lines to the Ringbahnhof. For reasons given below, these plans were not implemented, but they dictated the sharp curves and severe gradients in this section of the tunnel, and generations of passengers have had to endure the screaming of the wheels on these curves ever since!

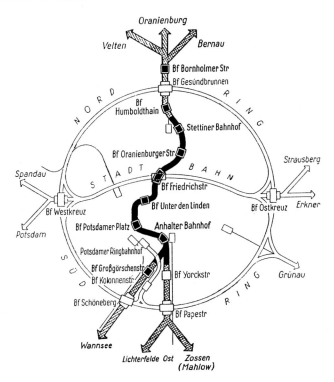

The next obstacle placed in the way of completion was the publication, on 30 January 1937, of the government's plans for the rebuilding of Berlin to fit it to be the capital of the 'thousand year empire'. Naturally, the railways had to adapt their own plans to suit the grand design and the proposal for two new terminal stations in the north and south of the central area, to be linked by tunnel, had a knock-on effect on the S-Bahn, as had the planned north-south triumphal road. The first new proposal was for an underground link to the Görlitzer Bahnhof, to leave the north-south line by a flying junction at the north end of Anhalter Bahnhof station and the second was for a widening and extension of the tunnel section at the southern portal, to serve the new south station. Quite a considerable amount of rebuilding of the new construction had to be undertaken and by that time, a shortage of labour in the construction industry had begun to make itself felt throughout Germany. It was not until 5 April 1939 that the service was extended to Potsdamer Platz and the line was connected to the southern lines south of their termini on 9 October 1939 (to Wannsee) and 6 November 1939 (to Lichterfelde). The formal opening ceremony was performed by Dr Dorpmüller, Minister of Transport, at Potsdamer Platz station on 8 October 1939. However, it was to be a further 52 years before the Nordsüdbahn operated in normal conditions.

In connection with the opening of the tunnel for through service, the Dresdener Bahn was electrified from Priesterweg to Mahlow on 15 May 1939 and further south to Rangsdorf on 6 October 1940. The proposed link to Görlitzer Bahnhof was not built, though some of the constructed tunnel still exists and the plans explain the present three through tracks layout in Anhalter Bahnhof S-Bahn station.

The new plans for the capital also envisaged a doubling of the extent of the S-Bahn services. Despite the outbreak of war, some work was undertaken on these plans, but the only visible effect on the S-Bahn was the provision of separate tracks between Mahlsdorf and Strausberg and a short extension from Lichterfelde Ost to Lichterfelde Süd, opened on 9 August 1943. Further extension of this line to Stahnsdorf via Teltow did not proceed beyond the necessary earthworks.

The route from Priesterweg to Lichterfelde Ost reopened at the end of May 1995, with the section to Lichterfelde Süd planned for mid-1997. The pre-war plans to extend this service to Stahnsdorf are, however, now long forgotten. A four-car train of class 480 stock arrives at Lichterfelde Ost on 27th June 1995. *Brian Hardy*

The S-Bahn network now had a route length of almost 295 km, of which 226.4 km was on separate track and only 68.61 km had to be shared with other trains. That it was one of Europe's finest suburban networks was shown by the growth in passenger numbers, from 358-million in 1927 to 512-million, 34.8% of all city traffic, in 1937. Wartime conditions further inflated this to 737-million in 1943, the last year of normal operation.

From Total War to Stand Null

The first air raids which seriously affected the S-Bahn were those of 23 November 1943, as a result of which the curve from Potsdamer Ringbahnhof was put out of action and from that date, for the first time in its history, the Ring was operated as a complete circle. Hitherto, trains on the Ringbahn ran Papestrasse – Potsdamer Ringbahnhof – Schöneberg (clockwise) and Schöneberg – Potsdamer Ringbahnhof – Papestrasse (anticlockwise). Services were interrupted many times in 1944 but it was always possible to effect repairs and a full service was still operating early in 1945. From then on, increasing coal shortages and, later, artillery bombardment, made it increasingly difficult to run any trains at all, and what services remained petered out altogether on 25 April 1945.

The greatest disaster to affect the network took place in the very last days of the war, when the entire Nordsüdbahn tunnel was flooded throughout its length and to a depth of several metres. The cause of this disaster has been the object of much speculation and the event has become sensationalised to the point where it has been difficult to distinguish fact from fiction. Given the circumstances of the last days of the war in Berlin, when the city no longer had a functioning government and when newspapers had ceased publication, this is perhaps not surprising. Whatever the reason for this disaster, all that can be said with certainty is that the tunnel was flooded, on or after 2 May 1945, probably as a result of the explosion in the bed of the Landwehrkanal and that up to 200 people may have died as a result. Whatever the cause, the tunnel, along with most of the remainder of the system, was unusable and no trains could be run. The S-Bahn had reached Stand Null – its nadir.

Reconstruction and Cold War

Given the state of the system at the capitulation of Germany, it is remarkable that by December 1945, some 216 km of the Berlin S-Bahn were again in operation, albeit in many places with single track only and by trains running shuttle rather than through services. The first train had run on 6 June 1945, from Wannsee inwards to Schöneberg and two months later the first central Berlin station – Potsdamer Ringbahnhof – was reopened. Trains returned to the Stadtbahn on 25 August and to the complete Ring on 8 February 1946. Fears of what might be lurking in the waters of the Nordsüdbahn tunnel had probably been the reason why the Russians had given early permission for work to begin on its reconstruction, which actually began on 25 May 1945. The underground station of Stettiner Bahnhof was in use again, initially as a terminus, from 31 January 1946 and a shuttle service from Anhalter Bahnhof to Friedrichstrasse followed from 2 June 1946. The tunnel was reopened throughout on 16 November 1947. The last part of the network to be brought back into service was the line to Erkner which, much as a single track, was reopened in stages during 1948, the last on 2 November. Many lines, particularly in the east, remained single track. Given the background of an occupied city and a collapsing currency, it was a most impressive performance.

The complete list of post-war S-Bahn reopenings is given on the next page.

Date	Section(s) of Line Reopened
6 June 1945	Wannsee–Schöneberg
9 June 1945	Spandau–Westkreuz
18 June 1945	Treptower Park–Papestrasse
11 July 1945	Schöneberg–Grossgörschenstrasse
11 July 1945	Westkreuz–Charlottenburg
11 July 1945	Papestrasse–Wilmersdorf
11 July 1945	Ostkreuz–Gesundbrunnen (via Schönhauser Allee)
11 July 1945	Neukölln–Grünau
11 July 1945	Ostkreuz–Biesdorf
19 July 1945	Stettiner Fernbahnhof–Schönholz
26 July 1945	Schöneweide–Spindlersfeld
28 July 1945	Halensee–Westend
31 July 1945	Biesdorf–Mahlsdorf
2 August 1945	Yorckstrasse–Südende/Mariendorf (now Attilastrasse)
6 August 1945	Grossgörschenstrasse–Potsdamer Ringbahnhof
13 August 1945	Stettiner Bahnhof–Tegel
17 August 1945	Südende–Lichterfelde Süd
18 August 1945	Schönholz–Oranienburg
25 August 1945	Charlottenburg–Zoologischer Garten
5 September 1945	Westend–Jungfernheide
6 September 1945	Zoologischer Garten–Tiergarten
8 September 1945	Mariendorf–Mahlow
9 September 1945	Jungfernheide–Beusselstrasse
16 September 1945	Tegel–Heiligensee
17 September 1945	Wannsee–Dreilinden
17 September 1945	Jungfernheide–Gartenfeld
29 September 1945	Beusselstrasse–Putlitzstrasse
1 October 1945	Gesundbrunnen–Wedding
1 October 1945	Mahlow–Rangsdorf
12 October 1945	Tiergarten–Bellevue
15 October 1945	Bellevue–Lehrter Stadtbahnhof
19 October 1945	Lehrter Stadtbahnhof–Friedrichstrasse
4 November 1945	Friedrichstrasse–Alexanderplatz
5 November 1945	Schlesischer Bahnhof (now Hauptbahnhof)–Ostkreuz
15 November 1945	Alexanderplatz–Schlesischer Bahnhof (now Hauptbahnhof)
21 November 1945	Ostkreuz–Treptower Park
19 December 1945	Wedding–Putlitzstrasse
30 January 1946	Nordbahnhof–Humboldthain
15 February 1946	Treptower Park–Baumschulenweg
16 February 1946	Potsdam Stadt–Wannsee
2 June 1946	Friedrichstrasse–Anhalter Bahnhof
6 July 1946	Heiligensee–Velten
27 July 1946	Anhalter Bahnhof–Grossgörschenstrasse
15 August 1946	Anhalter Bahnhof–Yorckstrasse
15 July 1947	Spandau–Spandau West
16 November 1947	Nordbahnhof–Friedrichstrasse
5 January 1948	Ostkreuz–Köpenick
30 April 1948	Köpenick–Friedrichshagen
27 May 1948	Dreilinden–Stahnsdorf
1 September 1948	Friedrichshagen–Rahnsdorf
2 November 1948	Rahnsdorf–Erkner

Certain stations and sections of line deserve a mention in the S-Bahn history at this point. Stettiner Vorortbahnhof (Stettiner suburban station), located west of the main line station and opened on 20 December 1897, was used from 8 August 1924 for electric services. These were diverted into the North-South tunnel in 1936, with a four-track underground station, also known as Stettiner Bahnhof. This station was, of course, unusable after the flooding of the tunnel and the former Vorortbahnhof had also been damaged beyond repair. To allow a resumption of service to the northern suburbs, tracks in the main line station were electrified and services to Tegel began on 19 July 1945. These services reverted to the underground station on 31 January 1946. The station was renamed Nordbahnhof in 1950.

In the south, Potsdamer Fernbahnhof was the station used by express trains to Zehlendorf until wartime destruction, never being reinstated. Potsdamer Ringbahnhof, however, came back to life for services to Wannsee on 6 August 1945, but ceased on 27 July 1946 when Wannsee trains reverted to using the reopened north-south tunnel.

On the Ringbahn, the connections between Schöneberg and Papestrasse to Potsdamer Ringbahnhof were never re-established, nor the station of Kolonnenstrasse, adjacent to the Wannseebahn. Similarly the north curve between Charlottenburg and Witzleben never reopened. The southern curve between Charlottenburg and Halensee was reinstated after the Second World War, but for empty stock moves only.

The system which was thus returned to life, however, no longer served an un-divided city. The allies present at Yalta had decided to divide Berlin into three sectors, but the French later claimed their share, which had to be carved out of the area allocated to the western allies. The 20 pre-war districts of Berlin were therefore shared among four powers, the Russians taking eight, situated in the eastern part of the city, the pre-1933 base of the Communist party. The railways in this part of Germany went to the Russians and were later re-organised as Deutsche Reichsbahn, generally known as DR. This ensured that the S-Bahn remained under unified control, though the fixed installations in the western sectors were the responsibility of Verwaltung des ehemaligen Reichsbahn Vermögens in Berlin [West] – The Administration of the Property of the former Reichsbahn in Berlin [West]. Normally this was referred to as the VdeR. The fact that the S-Bahn continued to serve the entire city became progressively more important as street transport became confined to west or east. At the celebrations of 25 years of S-Bahn operation in August 1949, the posters on the stations proudly proclaimed "Über alle Sektorengrenzen hinweg rollt deine S-Bahn" (Your own S-Bahn runs across all the sector boundaries). As life returned to the city, Berliners depended even more on the system to provide city-wide communication.

This coverage also meant that the S-Bahn became embroiled in politics. The first occasion on which this led to considerable trouble occurred in 1949, with what in the west was called a strike and in the east the 'UGO Putsch'. West Berlin employees of DR were, from 1948, paid in eastern Mark but were obliged to pay all their basic living costs, such as rent, in western DM. At first, when the two currencies were at parity, this did not matter, but when the east Mark slid to a quarter of the value of the DM, these people found life difficult and naturally asked to be paid in DM. The management of DR refused, though, even if they had agreed, they would have had no means of paying in DM, since fares in all parts of the city were paid in east Mark. There was also increasing conflict between the official trade union, the Freier Deutsche Gewerkschaftsbund (FDGB) and the western breakaway union, the Unabbänigige Gewerkschaftsorganisation (UGO – Independent Workers' Organisation), which was not recognised by DR. The outcome was a strike, which began on 21 May 1949 and affected almost all the system, including most lines in the east, and also the newly instituted 'Inter Zone' trains. There was some physical violence, leading to one death at Zoologischer Garten. On 24 May the western allies ordered the occupation of railway property in West Berlin and this put an end to the violence, though the strike continued until 30 June and was only ended by diplomatic activity at the highest level. DR then agreed to pay West Berlin employees in DM and not to take any action against strikers. On 1 July 1949 the S-Bahn came back to life. During the strike, BVG had done its best to run a replacement bus service, with its own buses and some hired from the western allies and private operators. When services resumed, fares in West Berlin were charged in DM. The strike was the last occasion on which the eastern authorities tried directly to influence events in the west. From this time onwards, attention was given more to separating east from west.

Curiously, the Berlin Blockade of 1948/49 had not directly affected the S-Bahn, which had been able to maintain a full service throughout and carried in 1948 a post-war record number of passengers – 496 million.

When, on 1 June 1952, West Berliners were forbidden to enter the DDR without special permission, frontier controls had to be set up at stations where the S-Bahn crossed the city boundary, with much increased dwell time at these stations, and all outer suburban trains were cut back from West Berlin stations. In part replacement of these, electric S-Bahn services were extended to the following sections of line:

30 April 1951	Grünau – Königs Wusterhausen
7 July 1951	Lichterfelde-Süd – Teltow
3 August 1951	Spandau West – Staaken
14 August 1951	Spandau West – Falkensee
28 August 1951	Spandau – Jungfernheide

These works were undertaken in the course of a programme to eliminate the need for main line passenger and goods trains to traverse West Berlin, but they did also help traffic for the Festival of World Youth. Apart from the Ostbahnhof, all the main line termini fell out of use with the beginning of the summer timetable in May 1952. Using electrified goods lines between Pankow-Schönhausen and Schönhauser Allee, trains from Bernau diverted onto the eastern part of the Ring on 25 December 1952.

Also in 1952, certain politically sensitive groups in the DDR had been forbidden from contact with West Berliners. This was almost a physical impossibility for those who lived to the north and west and passed through West Berlin on their daily journeys to work in the eastern part of the city. To ensure that they could commute without fear of political corruption, through-running trains (Durchläuferzüge) were put into operation on 19 May 1953 – the trains, from Velten, Oranienburg, Potsdam and Falkensee ran, in theory, non-stop to the boundary to the first station in the Russian sector. There were two or three workings inwards in the morning peak and the same number outwards in the evening (midday on Saturdays). It was a severe operational headache trying to fit these trains in on a system which had always run on the basis of trains stopping at every station (except for the Bankers' Expresses), especially when most outer sections were still single track. In practice, they were often halted at signals and more than a few people took advantage of this to escape to West Berlin. To fill the place of the Durchläuferzüge within West Berlin, additional local workings had to be provided. Once work on the Outer Ring was complete, there was then no more need for the "Durchläuferzüge" and to almost universal relief, they disappeared from the timetable on 4 May 1958.

Another measure instituted to limit contact with the west was the practice of stabling as many trains as possible in the east overnight. This led to a great deal of empty train workings and the consequential 'dead' mileage. Railway staff in the east called the few trains that were still shedded in the west, 'Korea Trains', to indicate that they came from somewhere very far away!

There were also plans to institute control points at stations where the S-Bahn crossed the boundary with the Soviet sector and in connection with this, main line platform 'B' at Friedrichstrasse was electrified with a third rail in February 1953. There was a trial of the idea on 25 February, when all trains coming from West Berlin were terminated and passengers had to alight and go through controls before resuming their journey. But there were so many complaints from all sides, including the S-Bahn staff, (it would have become impossible to run any service on the Ring), that the idea was abandoned – for a while.

The DDR authorities then planned to institute sector controls at specially-built non-passenger platforms on the lines leading to the west at the following points on the Ring – between Schönhauser Allee and Gesundbrunnen, Treptower Park and Sonnen-allee and between Köllnische Heide and Baumschulenweg. Again, representations were made about the effect on the timetable and the plans were not adopted. Control, in a less strict form, was henceforth made at sector boundary stations within the limits of the timetable.

On 17 June 1953, mass demonstrations broke out in the eastern part of the city against new 'work norms' and abruptly at 10.55 all current was switched off, leaving many S-Bahn trains stranded. A few trains resumed running in the east on 18 June but it was not until 22 June that any service ran again in West Berlin and 9 July before full cross-sector services were resumed.

Despite all these alarms and excursions, the S-Bahn kept running, to provide an increasingly-valued city-wide service for Berliners. For management and staff, it was an almost impossible position – from the eastern authorities they were subject to almost constant political interference, while by the western allies, anxious to demonstrate their right to ownership of railway property, they were often prevented from making changes necessary to cope with the altered patterns of travel. That the services ran as well as they did was a great tribute to their professionalism.

Despite all this, there was also some progress. In the immediate post-war period, the extension to Strausberg, opened in 1944, was electrified in stages – Mahlsdorf to Hoppegarten on 7 March 1947, Hoppegarten to Fredersdorf on 1 September 1948 and through to the terminus on 31 October 1948. A shuttle service from Zehlendorf to Düppel was begun on 15 June 1948 and a new connection at Gesundbrunnen allowed trains from this area to reach Schöneweide workshops without the long detour that had hitherto been necessary. The Strausberg branch was further extended to Strausberg Nord on 1 January 1955, at first using diesel trains, with electrification following on 3 June 1956. This single-line extension served the DDR Ministry of Transport and a military base. Finally on 16 November 1958, the curve between Charlottenburg and Halensee, previously rebuilt but used only for empty stock transfers between the Stadtbahn and the Ring, was reopened for passenger service.

With these extensions, the total route length of the S-Bahn rose to 340 km, but much was still single-tracked and services were therefore limited by this. In the 1950s, about 420 million passengers used the S-Bahn each year. The system was valued by Berliners both for its intrinsic usefulness and as a unifying element in a more and more divided city.

All this came to an abrupt end on the night of 12/13 August 1961. During the evening, signalmen were surprised to find their boxes visited by rather secretive individuals, who clearly had no connection with the railways, while just after midnight reports began to come in of tracks being torn up on lines which crossed the boundary from West Berlin into the DDR, at places such as Lichtenrade and Teltow. Trains were terminated at sector boundary stations, such as Potsdamer Platz and West Berliners had to leave the stations and proceed on foot. Late travellers enjoying a last beer in the buffet were turned out abruptly, along with the staff. Above ground, troops were already beginning to erect a barrier of paving stones and barbed wire. On the following day, all trains from the east on the Stadtbahn were turned back at Friedrichstrasse, much to the surprise of passengers who had expected to be able to make a through journey. With the publication of an ordinance of the DDR Ministry of Transport, it became evident that Berlin was to be physically split into two cities.

Unfortunately, the boundaries of the Berlin boroughs were no more logical than those of London and the new frontier was tortuous and, in some places, definitely odd. In some streets, houses were in the west, while the pavement outside lay in the east. For the S-Bahn, the immediate consequence was the cessation of all services which ran into West Berlin from the east. This meant the closure of the links Pankow – Gesundbrunnen, Schönhauser Allee – Gesundbrunnen, Treptower Park – Sonnenallee, and Baumschulenweg – Köllnische Heide, reducing the Ring in the west to a shuttle service (between Gesundbrunnen and Sonnenallee/Köllnische Heide via Wilmersdorf). On the Stadtbahn all services from both east and west terminated at Friedrichstrasse, which had become a frontier station. The layout was altered to provide totally separate 'stations', the 'East' having the northern island platform, the 'West' having the middle island platform. In the station concourse, facilities for passport and visa control were installed. On the Nordsüdbahn, the stations Bornholmer Strasse, Nordbahnhof, Oranienburger Strasse, Unter den Linden and Potsdamer Platz were closed and sealed off by troops, while Wilhelmsruh, Schönholz and Wollankstrasse, which lay right on the boundary, could be used only by West Berliners.

Other sections of lines to cross the 'border' and close to S-Bahn services on 13 August 1961 were Lichtenrade – Rangsdorf (although a shuttle between Mahlow and Rangsdorf continued until early-September 1961), Lichterfelde Süd–Teltow, Wannsee–Stahnsdorf, Wannsee–Potsdam, Spandau West–Falkensee, Heiligensee–Hennigsdorf and Frohnau–Hohen Neuendorf. Two other short-lived shuttle services operated on the 'East' side of the border – between Potsdam and Griebnitzsee and between Falkensee and Albrechtshof, but only until 9 October 1961. A 'new' section of line opened on 10 December 1961 between Schönhauser Allee and Pankow, which replaced the section opened on 25 December 1952. The old tracks were the electrified main line tracks and were used to avoid traffic through West Berlin. After the construction of the Wall on 13 August 1961, this 'new' line was built swiftly to avoid S-Bahn and main line trains using the same tracks. The whole Schönhauser Allee–Pankow section was a border area and only one train was allowed at a time – trains were strictly forbidden to stop and Bornholmer Strasse station had previously been closed on 13 August 1961.

In the east, shuttle services were instituted on lines which had been cut and the service between Potsdam and East Berlin via the Outer Ring was strengthened, as was that from Bernau to the eastern part of the Ring. An S-Bahn shuttle service continued to operate between Velten and Stolpe-Süd (Hennigsdorf-Süd) until 15/16 August 1961, from when it was cut back to Hennigsdorf. This continued until it was taken over by DR a.c. trains on the morning of 21 September 1983 – the small S-Bahn depot at Velten survived until then. Services from Oranienburg were initially worked as a shuttle to Hohen Neuendorf until this could be re-routed – from 19 November 1961 back towards Pankow. The new connections were much longer than the lines they replaced and commuters had to spend much more time travelling on their daily journeys. After some confusion, services settled down to the new pattern.

As already mentioned, the only rail interchange point for passengers was at Friedrichstrasse, which is a three-level station. The deep level station area is served by U-Bahn line U6 while the north-south S-Bahn line is immediately above, and also in tunnel. West Berliners were able to interchange freely between them. The station above, located on the Stadtbahn viaduct with street exit into East Berlin, told a different story. It was divided into three parts – for main line trains, West Berlin S-Bahn trains and East Berlin S-Bahn trains. There was still free access between the West Berlin S-Bahn and the lower level S- and U-Bahn lines. The main line platforms were staffed by East German frontier guards, who were concerned only with trains going to or coming from the east. The platforms for East Berlin S-Bahn trains were physically separated by a high steel wall and platform access was only possible via the DDR frontier controls, often after a time-consuming process.

Within a few days, the anger felt by West Berliners at the division of the city, and the knowledge that the hard currency they paid to use the S-Bahn went straight into the DDR regime began to pose a new threat to its existence. On 17 August 1961 the Deutsche Gewerkschaftsbund Berlin, a branch of the German equivalent of the TUC, called for a complete boycott of the system in the west. Pickets at stations dissuaded would-be passengers and their arguments were backed up by posters with slogans such as "Jeder Westberliner S-Bahn Fahrgast bezahlt den Stacheldraht" *(Every West Berlin S-Bahn passenger is paying for the 'barbed wire')*, for that, at the beginning, is what it was – the solid concrete wall was to come later. The campaign was, and remained, brilliantly successful and passenger numbers shrank from 500,000 to around 100,000 per day. Maintaining the boycott called for some personal inconvenience on the part of West Berliners. Despite the Wall, it was still a big city and the distances from the outer suburbs, such as Frohnau, were considerable. The replacing buses took much longer than the trains and, especially for the elderly passengers, were less comfortable.

The S-Bahn, once the symbol of a modern and progressive city, had become a ghost system, on which almost empty trains stopped at increasingly dilapidated stations to set down and pick up little or no passengers before being waved on by unenthusiastic and unsmiling staff. Vandalism, first against fixed installations, later against the few travellers, grew and by 1970 the whole system exuded neglect, in total contrast to the smart U-Bahn trains and new buses of the BVG. In case anyone still felt like trying to find the S-Bahn, the U-Bahn had deleted all references to it from its maps, destination indicators and station signs, and locating a system which officially no longer existed required some persistence on part of the visitor to West Berlin. Relaxation of frontier controls in the 1970s brought a few more passengers to the Stadtbahn link to Friedrich-strasse, but against this, successive fare increases drove away some of the remaining business on other lines. By the 1970s, the west S-Bahn was carrying about 20–25 million passengers per year.

For West Berlin and the BVG, the boycott of the S-Bahn led to increasing depend-ence on the bus and, latterly, the private car, necessitating a considerable programme of building new roads and urban motorways. Buses had to be used for long journeys and the city's entire transport policy was deflected from rail to roads. The U-Bahn was extended – in some cases parallel to S-Bahn links – but such construction took time and the link on line U7 to Spandau, for example, was not completed until 1984. For the DR, charged with running these S-Bahn ghost trains, with staff paid at western rates, the financial nightmare grew, with deficits running at an annual average of DM 135-million by the mid-1970s. There were several attempts to interest the Senate of West Berlin in some kind of financial arrangement, but the latter body took refuge in the legal point that, while DR had rights of operation, the ownership of the lines in question belonged to the three Western allied forces, and that any such arrangement would require the agreement of the latter. In practice, the Senate, lukewarm about the S-Bahn, made no attempt to reach any such agreement. In the meantime, DR stopped recruitment and existing staff regularly found themselves working a 56-hour week.

In 1980 it was proposed that, with effect from 28 September, there would be considerable reductions in service. By that time, the S-Bahn's share of public transport in West Berlin had fallen to just 5%. To the staff, already dissatisfied with wage levels and conditions of service, this was the last straw and on 17 September 1980, DR staff quite spontaneously went on strike – only the section between Zoologischer Garten and Friedrichstrasse was operational. Not only the S-Bahn but also the container terminals were involved. The strike lasted for almost a week, during which the strikers made another approach to the Senate to suggest a take-over of the S-Bahn, with exactly the same result as previously. When it was over, the services were reduced even beyond the original proposals. Sections closed on 28 September 1980 were Gesundbrunnen – Sonnenalle/Köllnische Heide via Westend and Halensee (i.e. the remainder of the Ring), Charlottenburg – Halensee, Jungfernheide – Gartenfeld, Anhalter Bahnhof – Wannsee (this route was still used for depot trips to and from Wannsee), Zehlendorf – Düppel, Westkreuz – Staaken (via Olympia Stadion and Spandau) and Jungfernheide – Spandau West. Of the entire West Berlin network therefore, all that continued to see a service were the Nordsüdbahn (Heiligensee to Lichterfelde-Süd and Frohnau to Lichtenrade), and the Stadtbahn from Wannsee to Friedrichstrasse. The route length had been almost exactly halved, from 144.8 km to 72.2 km and only 38 out of 78 stations remained in service. As a result, about 300 staff were made redundant.

The S-Bahn Under BVG Administration 1984–1989

The strike had brought the S-Bahn back into the public eye and many now began to say that such a potentially useful link should not be allowed to wither away for purely political reasons. The topic was widely canvassed during the local elections of 1981 and in June 1982 the Senate finally agreed to initiate discussions for taking over the existing network plus the Wannseebahn. After prolonged negotiation with the government in Bonn, and with the agreement of the western allies, discussions with DR were begun in October 1983. These moved forward quickly and, again with allied consent, an agreement was signed on 30 December 1983.

This provided that, with effect from 03.00 on 9 January 1984, the S-Bahn lines in West Berlin should pass to the control of the Senate, together with 119 two-car trains. The section of line from Lehrter Stadtbahnhof to Friedrichstrasse would continue to be operated by DR, to whom a yearly payment of DM 1.1-million would be made.

As the Senate had no experience of running a railway, operation would be handed over to the BVG, who were not altogether pleased to have to administer a former competitor which they had pronounced dead some years back. Nor did they have much time for preparation. The sections of line which were out of service remained under legal ownership of the VdeR. However, despite reservations, BVG duly operated its first S-Bahn train shortly after 04.00 on 9 January 1984 from Charlottenburg to Lehrter Stadtbahnhof. An official ceremony followed at a later and somewhat more civilised hour. Only the Stadtbahn east of Charlottenburg, together with the section from Anhalter Bahnhof to Lichtenrade was operated, a total route length of only 21.2 km. At the same time, therefore, the sections Schönholz–Heiligensee, Priesterweg–Lichterfelde Süd, Anhalter Bahnhof–Frohnau and Charlottenburg–Wannsee all closed. It was not quite Stand Null again, but it was not far from it!

The first proposals envisaged only a very limited and gradual reopening of closed lines which seemed to suggest that the Senate remained half-hearted about the S-Bahn. However, protests evidently brought about a change of official opinion and on 1 May 1984 services were resumed between Charlottenburg and Wannsee and between Anhalter Bahnhof and Gesundbrunnen. The latter was further extended northwards to Frohnau of 1 October 1984, this section having been subject to a fairly extensive rebuilding. By now there were 53 km in operation and about 50,000 passengers a day were using the services. Meanwhile, the Wannseebahn was being extensively rehabilitated and the VdeR was working on the station buildings with particular care, many of which now enjoyed 'listed' status. Services on this line between Anhalter Bahnhof and Wannsee resumed on 1 February 1985, bringing the network total to 71.5 km. The legal basis of operation was also changed and the system was at first operated under a Prussian light railway Act of 1892 and later under the Federal German Railway Act of 1951. It was fortunate that ideas of putting the S-Bahn on the same legal footing as the U-Bahn were not adopted, as reunification would then have been a rather more complicated legal process.

In July 1984 the Senate published a transport plan in which the S-Bahn was to play a prominent part, with a consequent restructuring of the bus network to limit it to a feeder role to the S- and U-Bahn. During the next few years, much work was undertaken to bring the system, which had been neglected for so many years, up to contemporary standards. The section to Frohnau received double track, to allow the introduction of a 10-minute headway. This very complete rebuilding was not without both technical and environmental problems. Many trees and bushes had grown up on the disused track beds since 1945 and there were protests from environmentalists when these were cut down. The years 1986–87 saw the complete rebuilding of the stations Anhalter Bahnhof and Lehrter Stadtbahnhof, with the former restored to its original glory. This programme was carried out in connection with the celebrations marking the city's 750th anniversary. The tracks and bridges of the Stadtbahn were also thoroughly rebuilt. In 1988 the doubling of the section from Marienfelde to Lichtenrade was begun. Despite all this progress, it was made clear that there would be no further reopenings before the mid-1990s and many Berliners expressed dissatisfaction at this protracted timescale. This disapproval may have been one of the reasons for the election of a 'Red-Green' Senate at the local elections of 1989. The new Senate doubled the finance for the S-Bahn and proposed an accelerated timetable for reopenings, which were to be completed by 1994. Work on the reconstruction of the Ring began in 1989. By this time, 48-million passengers were using the service in a year.

Before the new plans could be realised, the demise of the DDR regime and the opening of the Wall on 9 November 1989 totally altered the political background and opened up a different future for the entire S-Bahn network.

The S-Bahn In East Berlin 1961–1989

While the fortunes of the system in the west were in decline, the S-Bahn in the east was enjoying official favour and a period of prosperity. The U-Bahn served only a small part of East Berlin and the S-Bahn therefore had to be the backbone of the city's transport system. The closure of the central termini made it necessary to develop the station of Berlin-Lichtenberg as a main line station and the S-Bahn therefore also acquired a feeder function to the main line trains of the DR.

The first extension was necessitated by the closure of the line from Oranienburg. The Outer Ring, which had been gradually developed in the 1950s, was provided with separate S-Bahn tracks between Bergfelde and Hohen Neuendorf and a new service was instituted on 19 November 1961, linking Hohen Neuendorf with Blankenburg. The airport of Berlin Schönefeld was being developed at this time and the short branch from Grünauer Kreuz was electrified on 26 February 1962. The airport station also became an important interchange with main line trains. The S-Bahn in the east now had a route length of 165.3 km.

At the beginning of the 1970s, plans were drawn up for a new suburb at Marzahn, to house 100,000 people. To serve this, a new branch of the S-Bahn was built from

Friedrichsfelde Ost to Ahrensfelde. This left the main line by a flyover at Biesdorf. Services began as far as Marzahn on 30 December 1976 and was extended to Otto-Winzer-Strasse (now Mehrower Allee) on 15 December 1980. The last short section to Ahrensfelde opened for traffic on 30 December 1982, by which time the entire new line had double track. This was the first section of the S-Bahn to be built in conjunction with the planned development of a new part of the city and it has enjoyed excellent patronage.

Another new housing development was meanwhile taking place in Wartenberg and a new line was constructed to serve it. Branching away beyond Springpfuhl, Hohen-schönhausen was reached on 20 December 1984 and on to Wartenberg exactly a year later.

During the 1970s there were increasing problems of capacity on the northern part of the Outer Ring, which had to be shared by S-Bahn and main line trains. Electrification of the latter at 15kV with overhead current collection made it essential to separate the two. Over the 10 km stretch between Schönfliess and Karower Kreuz, separate tracks for S-Bahn trains were brought into use on 2 September 1982, thus allowing Oranien-burg trains to have their own tracks throughout. Some of this 10 km route is single track and provision has been made for future stations at Arkenberge and Buchholz Nord, should future housing developments materialise. Electrification of the line to Falkensee also brought problems in Birkenwerder station, where these trains shared a platform with the S-Bahn and here a transformer was required to allow this practice to continue, coming into operation in October 1983. There could also have been problems on the section between Hennigsdorf and Velten and, to avoid vast expense, the shuttle service over this section, which had operated since 1961, was converted briefly to diesel traction before going over to 15kV operation on 7 October 1983. However, the third rail returned to this section in 1987 when the former second track of the Kremmener Bahn was provided with a third rail, to allow testing of new S-Bahn trains built by LEW (now AEG) Hennigsdorf.

Other sections of the network were rebuilt with double track, as between Birken-werder and Lehnitz in 1963–64 and Grünau and Zeuthen in 1979–80 and by 1989, only 48.2 km of single track remained in service. Today, the sections of line still single-tracked are as follows:

Line	At/Between
S1	A small section south of Oranienburg station
S1	Hohen Neuendorf – Frohnau
S2	Lichtenrade – Blankenfelde with passing loop at Mahlow
S25	Tegel – Schönholz with passing loop between Karl-Bonhoeffer-Nervenklinik and Alt-Reinickendorf
S3/7	Wannsee – Potsdam Stadt with passing loops at Griebnitzsee and Babelsberg
S46	Zeuthen – Königs Wusterhausen
S5	Hoppegarten – Strausberg Nord with passing loops at Fredersdorf and Strausberg
S8	Buch – Bernau with passing loop at Zepernick
S10	East of Schönfleiss – east of Mühlenbeck-Mönchmühle
S10	Schöneweide – Spindlersfeld
–	Connection between Charlottenburg (on the Stadtbahn) and Halensee (on the Ringbahn)

These extensions and improvements resulted in a growth of passenger numbers, which had reached a post-war record of 242-million in 1965. Redundant trains were transferred from the west to cope with this increase. Thereafter, numbers declined slowly as the growth of private transport, usually in the form of a 'Trabant', became noticeable even in East Berlin, and reached a nadir of 158-million in 1983. The extensions of the 1980s reversed this trend and by 1989 the total of 178-million passengers was reached.

In 1988 DR began construction of an extension of the line beyond Wartenberg as far as Sellheimbrücke, a distance of 4 km. On 1 July 1989, the first cross-platform interchange with the U-Bahn was provided at Wuhletal when the extension of the latter to Hönow reached that point – it had in fact been originally proposed to build this line as part of the S-Bahn, but increasing problems of track and station capacity in the inner area prevented this.

Thus by 1989, the S-Bahn, responsible for almost half of all local transport in East Berlin, was once again providing excellent service. Modernised stations and trains and, latterly, new trains, suggested a new future for it. The sudden political changes, however, meant that the future was to be somewhat different from that which had been envisaged.

Reunification 1989–1995

The immediate effect of the opening of the DDR frontier on the evening of 9 November 1989 was a severe crisis of capacity on all BVG services, especially S-Bahn line S3, Friedrichstrasse-Wannsee, since most visitors from the east made for the Kurfürstendamm, easily reached from Zoologischer Garten (Zoo) station. To help out, DR transferred two full (eight-coach) sets on loan to the West on the night of 10/11 November. When split to run with BVG stock as two coach sets, these were normally placed in the centre of a train, but complete trains of DR stock were also operated. Although of the same design as the BVG trains, they had to return east after two weeks use, since spare parts kept in BVG workshops were of western manufacture and unsuited to these trains. DR staff, horrified at the amount of graffiti with which trains in the west were covered, were probably glad not to let their own stock stay away from home for too long! An all-night service, on a 20-minute headway, was instituted on line S3. Line S1 was also extended from Anhalter Bahnhof to Gesundbrunnen, and also enjoyed a night service. Services in the east were under pressure as people made for the border crossings and for several days a peak-hour service was provided at all times. A supplementary service was also run between Treptower Park and Schönefeld, from which there was a new bus service into West Berlin. Gradually the torrent of visitors slowed to a steady trickle, but extra trains were still run at weekends until well into 1990. The last DR sets were returned east in February 1990.

The above is a very brief summary of the most hectic weeks in the history of public transport in Berlin, but no bare recitation of facts and figures can attempt to convey the excitement and hope of these weeks, when staff worked long hours to take crowds there and back, and when these crowds themselves patiently waited in rows on station platforms, knowing that four or five trains might have to pass before they could hope to board one.

Because of the track alterations which had been made in 1961, it was not at first possible to operate through east-west services on a regular basis, though some specials were operated. The first through west-east S-Bahn trains to carry passengers over the Stadtbahn and through Friedrichstrasse to Marx-Engels-Platz (now Hackescher Markt) was provided as early as 11 December 1989, to take children from Charlottenburg to a concert in the Palast der Republik.

On 1 March 1990, Senator Nagel presented the plans of the Senate for the reopening of closed cross-border sections at a press conference appropriately held at Bornholmer Strasse station. The first trains to call there since August 1961 stopped at a hastily-cleared platform at 11.17 on that date, although it was to be another nine months before normal passenger usage could be reinstated. Included in the plans was the development of Bornholmer Strasse station as an interchange station between the two networks with a new platform on the eastern line from Pankow to Schönhauser Allee and a temporary footbridge to connect this with the existing station. The other lines in the programme were Lichtenrade–Mahlow, Köllnische Heide–Baumschulenweg, Frohnau–Hohen Neuendorf and Wannsee–Griebnitzsee. The total cost of restoring services to 22.3 km of route and rebuilding Bornholmer Strasse station was estimated to be around DM 450-million.

Meanwhile, DR had instituted a shuttle service with four-coach double-deck stock and diesel hydraulic locomotives between Potsdam Hauptbahnhof and Wannsee. This first regular service between the two sections of the S-Bahn was inaugurated by the Lord Mayor of Potsdam and the Mayor of Zehlendorf when a train reached Wannsee at 05.59 on 22 January 1990. Out of respect for the sleeping inhabitants of the area, the BVG band did not take part in these early-morning festivities. The trains ran approximately hourly and frontier controls were carried out at Griebnitzsee. This station was also opened for boarding and alighting passengers at the same time, having been closed to these since 13 August 1961. It was, however, used as a control station for main line trains between West Berlin and the Federal Republic of Germany.

Work was also undertaken to reinstate the connection at Friedrichstrasse and regular through services began in the very early hours (03.49) of 2 July 1990, the day after the currency union had come into force. Despite the early hour, many enthusiasts turned out to participate in this historic occasion, the darkness being illuminated by sparks from the collector shoes and by sparklers inside the train! A formal reopening, attended by the Mayors of the two parts of the city and enlivened by the brass band of DR, took place at a (slightly) more civilised time of 06.21, when Director Lorenzen of BVG signalled off a train from Wannsee to Königs Wusterhausen. A few minutes later, President Möller of DR Berlin waved off the corresponding train in the opposite direction. For Berliners, this resumption of through service on the Stadtbahn marked the coming reunification of the city. Border controls, which in the last months were purely a formality, were ended in the last days of June 1990 and the checkpoints at Friedrichstrasse were removed, as was the dividing partition between the two S-Bahn platforms. It is perhaps now hard to appreciate that trains departing within a few yards of each other, separated by a high and solid wall, in fact belonged to separate countries. Also, on 2 July 1990, Oranienburger Strasse on the Nordsüdbahn was reopened for traffic, followed on 1 September by Unter den Linden and Nordbahnhof, and on 22 December 1990 by Bornholmer Strasse. A provisional 'halt' on the eastern network at this point was brought into use on 5 August 1991, with interchange at street level via the girder bridge carrying the street of the same name.

With the reunification on 3 October 1990, both DR and the VdeR passed to the control of the Federal Minister of Transport, though almost alone of ex-DDR institutions, the former continued in existence until 1 January 1994, when it was merged with Deutsche Bundesbahn, under the title of Deutsche Bahn AG, normally referred to as DBAG. However, because of financial decisions already taken, it was decided to leave the BVG-operated section with what was now the Land of Berlin until the same date. On 1 January 1994, therefore, the entire S-Bahn network was finally reunited and municipal operation of the western lines came to an end a few days short of ten years. In fact, during the period 1991–94, there was very close co-operation between the two operators and joint services on the Stadtbahn worked smoothly. BVG drivers did not work trains east of Friedrichstrasse, but DR staff operated through to the west. This co-operation resulted in a large number of improvements being effected before formal reunification took place. The Nordsüdbahn was completely renovated over a period of several months in 1991 – the northern section was closed from 2 April to 5 August and the southern section from then until 1 March 1992. As the line had not had a proper overhaul since the flooding of 1945, the renovation work was extensive, involving the tunnels, track, power supply and signalling, at a cost of DM 58-million.

The renovation of the Nordsüdbahn enabled the long-closed Potsdamer Platz station to be reopened from 1 March 1992, although with very temporary facilities. Until modernisation work of the station proper commences in the future, there is but one platform for each direction instead of the two islands in use up to 1961. For the time being, the station and platform walls comprise aluminium sheeting acting as hoardings, with the access to the street comprising very temporary wooden stairs. All this led out (in 1994) to an almost deserted wasteland, still with some abandoned S-Bahn station entrances. The only activities there then were a man selling bits from what remained of the Wall and two high towers providing 'bungee-jumping' facilities. It is a sobering thought recalling that the Potsdamer Platz area used to be the 'Piccadilly Circus' of Berlin! In the summer of 1995, however, much had changed at street level. Gone is the man selling pieces of the wall and much of the surrounding area has been transformed into a huge building site with countless crane jibs occupying the sky line. The complete plans for the Potsdamer Platz area can be seen on display painted on a huge circular canvas in an exhibition rotunda near the existing station. For the station itself, Potsdamer Platz S-Bahn station is being completely rebuilt and is to have an impressive 50x50-metre glass 'cube' entrance.

In the suburbs, priority was given to restoring a through service from Wannsee to Potsdam, now the capital of the new Land of Brandenburg. After some prodding on the part of the Ministry of Transport, this came into operation on 1 April 1992 using single track with one passing loop – trains ran every 20 minutes. A full service, on a 10-minute daytime headway, followed in the summer of 1993 with passing loops operational at both the intermediate stations of Griebnitzsee and Babelsberg.

In northern Berlin, the line between Frohnau and Hohen Neuendorf was reopened on 31 May 1992 with services on the 1961 link line being correspondingly reduced. In the south, on 31 August 1992, the connection from Lichtenrade to Blankenfelde was restored. Modernised double-deck DR stock on regional line R2 provided a connection to Schönefeld.

Meanwhile, work continued on the rehabilitation of the southern and western part of the Ring. In fact, this was more than simple rehabilitation, since stations needed total rebuilding or, in some cases, such as Wilmersdorf, moved to a new location, to improve interchange with other modes of transport. These improvements increased the cost of this project by almost 50% above the planned level of DM 600-million and led to some criticism of its being a luxury programme. Finally, services were restored on 17 December 1993, when two trains of new class 485 stock ran in parallel from Baumschulenweg to Westend. The service was actually operated by DR on behalf of BVG until the formal assumption of responsibility on 1 January 1994. Until the reconstruction of the whole Ring has been completed, services currently operate alternately to Flughafen Schönefeld and Königs Wusterhausen, giving a 10-minute service on the Ring itself. Such was the popularity of the Ring that soon after reopening, from the summer of 1994, additional peak shuttles were introduced between Baumschulenweg and Halensee, doubling the service on this section, and extended yet again in 1995 from Halensee to Westend.

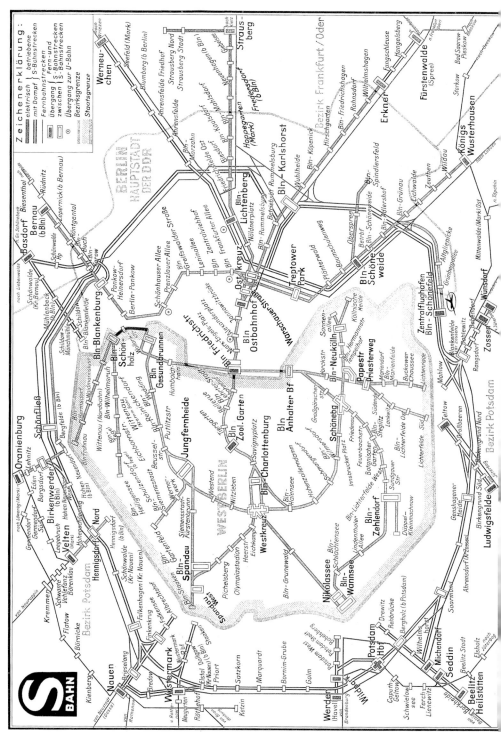

In 1994, DBAG, formerly DR, began a rather more modest rebuilding of the northern section of the Ring, from Westend to Schönhauser Allee, but also including alterations in the areas of Gesundbrunnen and Bornholmer Strasse, to allow through services to operate in the future between the Ring and northern lines. These connections, to be known as Nordkreuz and to be opened in stages, should all be operational by 1999, when the Ring will once again be open throughout. Before then, however, the section from Westend to Jungfernheide should reopen in mid-1997 and from Jungfernheide to Westhafen (Putlitzstrasse) in mid-1998. Around the south-eastern side of the Ring, Neukölln to Treptower Park is expected to reopen by the end of 1997.

Work has also continued on two projects begun by DR before reunification, namely the doubling of S-Bahn tracks between Mahlsdorf and Hoppegarten including a new station at Birkenstein, and the completion of the extension of the Wartenberg line to Sellheimbrücke, although the latter project is unlikely to see the much traffic for a few years and further extension is problematic.

Resumption of services on the branch to Heiligensee has caused more financial wrangling than has been the case with any other line and has also been delayed while possible future electrification at 15kV has been considered. Finally, when the Berlin Senate had agreed to meet the cost of removing the third rail installations in the event of future electrification at 15kV and that of laying down a separate line for goods trains on part of this section, work was begun in 1994 on the section as far as Tegel, with a possible later extension to Heiligensee. The first stage of reopening, from Schönholz to Tegel (7.07 km) was achieved on 28 May 1995, and on 14 August 1995 work began on the section northwards from Tegel. This should reopen as far as Heiligensee in mid-1997 and on to Hennigsdorf in December 1997. The line will be single-tracked with a passing loop at Heiligensee. Work has also progressed on the line from Priesterweg to Lichterfelde Ost (4.13 km) and this, too, opened on 28 May 1995. Work was scheduled to begin in November 1995 on reconstructing the 2.29 km line to Lichterfelde-Süd, for reopening in mid-1997 but the remaining 2.51 km to Teltow is unlikely to reopen.

Work began in 1994 on the reconstruction and rehabilitation of the cross-city Stadt-bahn viaduct. For the period of rebuilding, expected to take until May 1997, the main line trains between Zoologischer Garten and Hauptbahnhof were withdrawn from 3 October 1994. The main line tracks have been equipped for S-Bahn services, diverted over these tracks from 31 October 1994. As certain intermediate stations on this section do not have platforms on the main line alignment, a temporary platform for eastbound S-Bahn trains has been opened at Hackescher Markt, while Jannowitzbrücke, Tiergarten and Bellevue stations closed completely for rebuilding on 28 October 1994 and will remain so until reconstruction is completed. It is expected that S-Bahn trains will reassume their original tracks in 1996, from when the Fernbahn (main line) tracks will be reconstructed and electrified at 15kV overhead.

In the future it is anticipated to reopen the branch from Westkreuz to Spandau (8 km) by 1999, in connection with the construction of a high-speed line to Hannover. Work on this has already started and in July 1995 old tracks had been cleared and new canopies were noted being constructed at Olympia Stadion. However, this station is unlikely to be rebuilt on the grand scale it had in 1936, with its eight terminating tracks and platform faces, as well as the two through tracks for the normal service to and from Spandau. Other lines with possibilities of reopening, as yet without a projected date, is the branch from Jungfernheide to Gartenfeld (4.46 km) and the section from Spandau to Falkensee (8.80 km).

Station Renamings

The number of stations renamed on the Berlin S-Bahn is many and varied, most often for political reasons. Those that could be ascertained are listed as follows:

Present Lines	Opened	Name	Date Renamed	Renamed
S1, S3, S7	01.06.1874	Wannensee	15.05.1879	Dreilinden (Wannsee)
			Jan–1884	**Wannsee**
S1	01.11.1904	Zehlendorf Beerenstrasse	15.12.1911	Zehlendorf West
			28.09.1958	Lindenthaler Allee
			07.03.1987	**Mexikoplatz**
S1	22.09.1838	Zehlendorf	15.12.1911	Zehlendorf Mitte
			01.10.1938	**Zehlendorf**
S1	15.12.1872	Lichterfelde	01.09.1886	Gross-Lichterfelde
			01.01.1899	Gross Lichterfelde West
			21.03.1925	**Lichterfelde West**
S1	13.06.1839	Steglitz	31.05.1992	**Rathaus Steglitz**
S1	09.10.1939	Grossgörschenstrasse	31.05.1992	**Yorckstrasse (Grossgörschenstrasse)**
S1, S2	28.07.1936	Stettiner Bahnhof	01.12.1950	**Nordbahnhof**
S1, S2	10.07.1877	Prinzenallee	15.10.1879	Pankow (Prinzenallee)
			1880–1892	Prinzenallee (Pankow)
			Not known	Pankow
			Not known	Pankow (Prinzenallee)
			Not known	Pankow (Wollankstraße)
			Aug–1893	Pankow (Nordbahn)
			01.05.1911	Pankow Nordbahn
			03.10.1937	**Wollankstrasse**
S1, S2	10.07.1877	Reinickendorf	15.10.1878	Schönholz (Reinickendorf)
			1884	Schönholz – Reinickendorf
			15.05.1938	**Schönholz**
S1, S2	10.07.1877	Rosenthal	Not known	Reinickendorf, Rosenthalerstrasse
			Not known	Strasse Nach Rosenthal
			Not known	Reinickendorf, Rosenthaler Strasse
			03.10.1937	**Wilhelmsruh**
S1, S2	10.07.1877	Dalldorf	01.01.1906	Wittenau (Nordbahn)
			01.05.1911	Wittenau Nordbahn
			24.09.1994	**Wittenau (Wilhelmsruher Damm)**
S1	10.07.1877	Hermsdorf	1886	Hermsdorf i Mark
			01.05.1911	Hermsdorf bei Berlin
			06.10.1929	**Hermsdorf**
S1	01.05.1910	Frohnau (Mark)	01.02.1938	**Frohnau**
S1, S10	01.09.1877	Hohen-Neuendorf	01.05.1911	Hohen Neuendorf
			Jun–1928	**Hohen Neuendorf (bei Berlin)**

Present Lines	Opened	Name	Date Renamed	Renamed
S1, S10	10.07.1877	Birkenwerder	01.05.1911	Birkenwerder (Bezirk Potsdam)
			Sep–1927	**Birkenwerder (bei Berlin)**
S2	01.05.1903	Yorkstrasse	Nov–1909	**Yorckstrasse**
S2	15.02.1895	Mariendorf	31.05.1992	**Attilastrasse**
S2	08.10.1950	Blankenfelde (Kreis Teltow)	17.05.1953	**Blankenfelde (Kreis Zossen)**
S25	01.10.1893	Reinickendorf (Dorf)	01.05.1911	Reinickendorf
			28.05.1995	**Alt-Reinickendorf**
S25	01.10.1893	Dalldorf (Cremmener Bahn)	01.10.1893	Dalldorf (Kremmener Bahn)
			20.12.1893	Wittenau (Kremmener Bahn)
			28.05.1995	**Karl-Bonhoeffer-Nervenklinik**
S25	01.10.1893	Eichbornstrasse	28.05.1995	**Eichborndamm**
S25, S26	15.08.1880	Südende (Lankwitz)	01.10.1885	Südende – Lankewitz
			01.10.1899	**Südende**
S25, S26	01.12.1895	Lankwitz, Viktoriastrasse	01.10.1899	**Lankwitz**
S25, S26	01.10.1899	Gross Lichterfelde Ost	21.03.1925	**Lichterfelde Ost**
S3, S7	22.09.1938	Potsdam	02.10.1960	**Potsdam Stadt**
S3, S7	1862	Neuendorf	01.05.1890	Nowawes-Neuendorf
			01.03.1908	Nowawes
			01.04.1938	**Babelsberg**
S3, S7	01.06.1874	Neu-Babelsberg	Apr–1883	Neubabelsberg
			01.04.1938	Babelsberg – Ufastadt
			01.04.1949	**Griebnitzsee**
S3, S7	01.08.1879	Halensee (Hundekehle)	Not known	Halensee
			Not known	Hundekehle
			20.05.1884	**Grunewald**
S3, S7, S9, S75	10.12.1928	Ausstellung	15.01.1932	**Westkreuz**
S3, S5, S7, S75, S9	05.01.1885	Thiergarten	01.01.1904	**Tiergarten**
S3, S5, S7, S75, S9	07.02.1882	Lehrter Bahnhof	01.05.1911	**Lehrter Stadtbahnhof**
S3, S5, S7, S75, S9	07.02.1882	Börse	01.05.1951	Marx-Engels-Platz
			31.05.1992	**Hackescher Markt**
S3, S5, S7, S75, S9	23.10.1842	Frankfurter Bahnhof	Not known	Niederschlesisch – Märkischer Bahnhof *
			15.10.1881	Schlesischer Bahnhof
			01.12.1950	Ostbahnhof
			15.12.1987	**Hauptbahnhof**
S3, S5, S6, S7, S75, S8, S9, S10	07.02.1882	Stralau – Rummelsburg	15.05.1933	**Ostkreuz**

* Common name. Official name was Berliner Bahnhof der Niederschlesisch-Märkischen Eisenbahn.

Present Lines	Opened	Name	Date Renamed	Renamed
S3	01.06.1882	Kietz – Rummelsburg	01.10.1914	Rummelsburg bei Berlin
			15.03.1933	**Rummelsburg**
S3	15.05.1878	Sadowa	06.10.1929	**Wuhlheide**
S3	22.10.1842	Cöpenick	15.09.1933	**Köpenick**
S3	15.11.1892	Neu-Rahnsdorf	01.10.1902	**Wilhelmshagen**
S45, S46	15.11.1877	Charlottenburg – Westend	15.10.1881	**Westend**
S45, S46	13.11.1877	Grunewald	20.05.1884	**Halensee**
S45, S46	15.12.1883	Schmargendorf	17.12.1993	**Heidelberger Platz**
S45, S46	15.11.1877	Wilmersdorf	1881	Wilmersdorf – Friedenau
			15.05.1938	Wilmersdorf
			17.12.1993	**Bundesplatz**
S45, S46	01.01.1872	Rixdorf	05.03.1912	**Neukölln**
S46	13.09.1866	Königs-Wusterhausen	Not known	**Königs Wusterhausen**
S5	01.08.1944	Giebelsee	28.05.1967	**Petershagen Nord**
S5	15.09.1872	Petershagen	01.01.1875	Fredersdorf
			01.05.1911	Fredersdorf (Kreis Niederbarnim)
			Not known	**Fredersdorf (bei Berlin)**
S5	01.05.1870	Hoppegarten	01.05.1911	**Hoppegarten (Mark)**
S5	01.05.1911	Mahlsdorf (Kreis Niederbarnim)	06.12.1929	**Mahlsdorf**
S5	25.08.1869	Caulsdorf	15.10.1881	**Kaulsdorf**
S5, S7, S75	1881	Lichtenberg	10.11.1882	Lichtenberg – Friedrichsfelde
			15.05.1938	**Lichtenberg**
S5, S7, S75	01.10.1902	Rummelsburg Ost	01.10.1914	Neu-Lichtenberg
			12.12.1954	**Nöldnerplatz**
S6, S8, S9, S10	01.02.1875	Treptow	03.10.1937	**Treptower Park**
	15.06.1874	Adlershof	08.01.1894	Adlershof – Glienicke
			01.10.1901	Adlershof – Alt-Glienicke
			01.05.1911	Adlershof – Alt Glienicke
			01.01.1935	**Adlershof**
S6, S8, S9, S10, S45, S46	Jun–1868	Neuer Krug	15.05.1876	Bude 7 Johannisthal Neuer Krug
			1880	Johannisthal Niederschönweide
			07.07.1893	Johannisthal Niederschöneweide
			01.10.1895	Niederschöneweide – Johannisthal
			23.12.1908	Nieder – Schöneweide – Johannisthal
			01.05.1911	Niederschöneweide (Johannisthal)
			06.10.1929	**Schöneweide**
S6, S8, S46	Not known	Grünau	01.05.1911	Grünau (Mark)
			13.09.1966	**Grünau**

Present Lines	Opened	Name	Date Renamed	Renamed
S6, S46	01.06.1874	Schmöckwitz	01.07.1898	Eichwalde – Schmöckwitz
			01.02.1935	Eichwalde (Kreis Teltow)
			17.05.1953	**Eichwalde**
S6, S46	01.06.1874	Bude 21 Hankels Ablage	01.11.1897	**Zeuthen**
S7	15.12.1980	Otto-Winzer-Strasse	31.01.1992	**Mehrower Allee**
S7	15.12.1980	Bruno-Leuschner-Strasse	31.01.1992	**Raoul-Wallenberg-Strasse**
S7	28.09.1979	Karl-Maron-Strasse	31.01.1992	**Poelchaustrasse**
S8	01.09.1881	Zepernick (Kreis Niederbarnim)	17.05.1953	**Zepernick (bei Bernau)**
S8, S10	15.10.1880	Pankow – Schönhausen	03.10.1954	**Pankow**
S8, S10	01.02.1875	Weissensee	01.10.1946	Greifswalder Strasse
			16.04.1986	Ernst-Thälmann-Park
			31.05.1992	**Greifswalder Strasse**
S8, S10	01.05.1895	Landsberger Allee	22.04.1950	Leninallee
			31.05.1992	**Landsberger Allee**
S8, S10	04.05.1881	Central Viehhof	Not known	Zentral Viehhof
			Not known	**Storkower Strasse**
S8, S10	1872	Friedrichsberg	01.10.1897	Frankfurter Allee
			21.12.1949	Stalinallee
			14.11.1961	**Frankfurter Allee**
S9, S45	Autumn 1951	Schönefeld (Kreis Teltow)	26.02.1962	Schönefeld (bei Berlin)
			15.07.1962	**Flughafen Berlin-Schönefeld**

Abandoned Routes

Sections of line which are at present regarded as unlikely to reopen include Spandau–Staaken (4.68 km), Wannsee–Stahnsdorf (4.15 km), Jungfernheide– Spandau (6.17 km) and Zehlendorf–Düppel (2.51 km), all where traffic potential is considered low.

The various reopenings described earlier could possibly mark the last expansion of the 3rd-rail S-Bahn network and future extensions are more likely to be at 15kV with overhead current collection. Plans for main line trains envisage the construction of a new 'central' station on the site of the former Lehrter Bahnhof and a north-south tunnel. This may reactivate the plans of the 1930s of a connection from the Nordsüdbahn at Potsdamer Platz towards the north-west. However, the very high cost of this project makes its realisation a possibility rather than a probability.

Since 1 January 1995, in accordance with the government's plans for regionalisation, the S-Bahn has been administered by the S-Bahn Berlin GmbH (GmbH – Limited Company), with all rolling stock and depot staff transferring to the new company.

Gesundbrunnen, now serving lines S1, S2 and S25, seen in a rather derelict state in 1990. The platforms at immediate left are those of the former Ringbahn, closed in 1980, while those in the left background are still in service. *Nick Agnew*

The same scene but in 1995 with only the pair of platforms serving the present lines S1, S2 and S25 still remaining, with the rest of the area flattened in readiness for redevelopment. By 1999 it is hoped that the Ring will once again be in operation complete – after an absence of nearly 40 years. *Brian Hardy*

On the 'city' side of Gesundbrunnen in July 1995, a six-car train of class 480 stock on S1 passes an eight-car train of class 476 stock bound for Wannsee via the Nordsüdbahn. The site of the former main line tracks can be seen on the left, while the tracks of the closed Ring line are to the left of that and pass over in the background. *Brian Hardy*

The Wannseebahn traverses the south-west suburbs of Berlin and at one time comprised a second pair of electrified tracks for fast services operating the peak-hour 'Bankers Express' service. These occupied the area to the left, although the service was not restored after the Second World War. This view was taken at Feuerbachstrasse on 24 June 1993. *Steve Williams*

The second pair of tracks on the Wannseebahn continued as far as Zehlendorf, which station is seen here in June 1994. The platforms on the right were provided for the erstwhile fast services but were also used between 1948 and 1980 for the shuttle service to and from Düppel, but are now derelict and overgrown. A class 475 train pauses for passengers (and bicycles), heading for the northern terminus of Oranienburg. *Jeanne Hardy*

After 13 years of closure, part of the Ringbahn came back to life in December 1993, from Westend and via the southern section, joining the rest of the S-Bahn system at Baumschulenweg. An eight-car train of class 485 stock departs Halensee on 3 July 1995. Behind the train on the right can be seen the present single-line non-passenger connection to the Stadtbahn, which links Halensee and Charlottenburg. *Brian Hardy*

By the time of its closure in 1984, the route to Tegel and Heiligensee had an air of neglect about it, apart from maybe the station garden at Eichbornstrasse, which still appeared to be cared for in August 1983. *Brian Patton*

The same location after the line was re-opened as far as Tegel on 28 May 1995, as seen in July 1995 with a train of class 480 stock arriving. The station has been renamed Eichborndamm. *Brian Patton*

For over 28 years, the city of Berlin was divided by the Wall. In the western suburbs, three stations lay right on the boundary, as typified by Wollankstrasse, which was then only available to West Berliners. Looking east, the wall can be seen adjacent to the track on the right on 26 May 1986. *John Laker*

A similar view taken in June 1995. Apart from the removal of the Wall, enabling free access between East and West, not much has changed apart from the growth of foliage. *Jeanne Hardy*

Work is seen in progress in 1990 on the reconstruction of the Ringbahn at Westkreuz, whose platforms are above those of the Stadtbahn, but were still available for station access. *Nick Agnew*

The same area after reopening, with a train of class 485/885 stock on the left. The rebuilding of the Ringbahn enabled facilities for the disabled to be provided, such as the lift seen behind and to the left of the stairs. *Jeanne Hardy*

The reopened island platform of Innsbrucker Platz on the Ringbahn (lines S45 and S46), during a heavy thunderstorm during the evening of 29 June 1994. *Brian Hardy*

The Stadtbahn at Friedrich-strasse in June 1994 with a train of class 476 stock passing the signal cabin "Frio" (Friedrich-strasse, upper level). In the background can be seen the Fernsehturm (television tower), from which magnificent views of the city of Berlin (and the Stadtbahn!) can be had from the top. At the present time, the left-hand Stadtbahn tracks and infrastructure are being re-built with all S-Bahn services temporarily using the main line tracks on the right. *Jeanne Hardy*

The reconstruction of the Stadt-bahn is taking place between Zoologischer Garten and Haupt-bahnhof, with S-Bahn trains expected to revert to their normal alignment later in 1996. Four stations (Tiergarten, Bellevue, Hackescher Markt and Janno-witzbrücke) have been closed during rebuilding, but a tempor-ary platform has been provided at Hackescher Markt in the east-bound direction, from where this view was taken on 6 July 1995, with reconstruction tak-ing place on the left and with the temporarily closed station in the background. *Brian Hardy*

Reconstruction work on the Stadtbahn near Friedrichstrasse. *Capital Transport*

The present terminus of the Ringbahn is at Westend, where a train of class 485 stock is seen coming from the reversing sidings on 27 June 1994, forming a service on S46 to Königs Wuster-hausen. The next stage of the Ringbahn to reopen is from here to Jungfernheide by mid-1997, although it will not be before 1999 at the earliest that the Ring operates 'full circle' ('Vollring') again. *Brian Hardy*

When the southern part of line S2 reopened south of Lichtenrade to Blankenfelde on 31 August 1992, a new station was built at the latter, which terminated at a higher level than the main line tracks to the right. On that basis, it is unlikely that the S-Bahn will be extended to its former ter-minus of Rangsdorf, which is served by Regional suburban services. A train of class 475 stock, in need of some attention to its paintwork, stands in the single platform station. *Brian Hardy*

The abandoned line to Teltow reopened as far as Lichterfelde Ost on 28 May 1995, where a train of class 480 stock is seen on 27 June 1995, the stations having been rebuilt after lying derelict since 1984. The line beyond Lichterfelde Süd, however, has not seen a service since 1961 and no date has been set for reopening. *Jeanne Hardy*

When U-Bahn line U5 was extended east to Hönow in 1989, a joint station with S-Bahn line S5 was provided at Wuhletal, offering cross-platform interchange between them. At the 'country' end, the city-bound track passes over the U-Bahn, where a train of class 477 stock, heading for Charlottenburg, is seen. *Brian Hardy*

Rolling Stock

Trains on the S-Bahn are normally made up of four two-coach sets, this eight-coach formation being referred to as a "Vollzug" (complete train). Occasionally, as in the early days of BVG operation in the west, trains may be made up of six coaches, a "Dreiviertel" or four coaches "Halbzug" (half train). The minimum for operation is a two-coach set, known as a "Viertelzug" (quarter train) but this formation is rarely operated in passenger service.

The original stock used on the Ringbahn was of double deck design with end stair-case and this was also utilised on services on the Stadtbahn when it first opened. Possibly because of the lack of headroom, Berliners nicknamed these 'Japanese Trains'. However, this stock suffered from the Achilles heel of all such designs, in that loading and unloading was a slow process and therefore dwell time at stations was much too long. It was therefore soon banished to staff trains to and from the various workshops in Berlin and was replaced on suburban services by compartment stock. This was at first four-wheeled, but three-axle and, later, bogie stock was also used, normally in close-coupled formations. Stock of this kind was used on the electric service to Lichter-felde-Ost – although electrified, it was still heated by a coal stove! Some of the compartment stock had internal corridors, like the post-war design on the Southern Region of British Railways, but these were to the side rather than in the centre of the coach.

The Prototype Electric Trains

When it was decided to build new trains for the electrification of the northern lines, DRG ordered six prototype trains from four manufacturers to test different arrange-ments of doors, seating and electrical equipment. Each train consisted of ten coaches, which could be split to operate as two five-coach sets. Bogie motor coaches flanked three four-wheel trailers in sets A to E, but in train F the coaches were articulated. Set D, with doors to every seating bay, bore more than a passing resemblance to the Tait trains which had just entered service in Melbourne, while set C had no central gangway and set E had longitudinal seating. All were close-coupled with various types of coupling and all had sliding single-leaf doors, operated by passengers. When delivered in 1923, the sets were tested behind steam locomotives on the Stadtbahn and Wann-seebahn. Electrical equipment was fitted in 1924 and they were placed in service on the newly-electrified line to Bernau. All were scrapped in 1933.

The Bernau Class of 1924 (Later Class 169)

This class consisted of 17 half-trains, each being made up of two bogie motors flanking three two-axle trailers, as in the prototype trains. The use of two-axle vehicles made these trains out of date before they even entered service and they also suffered from poor acceleration, largely due to the weight of the motor coaches (46.6 tonnes). They were built by four manufacturers, two of whom had supplied prototype trains and the traction equipment, some of which was automatic and some semi-automatic, was also supplied by four firms – clearly DRG was still experimenting. At first they were painted dark green and received the red and ochre livery in 1929.

The trains entered service on the northern electrified routes in 1924 and ran on these until the opening of the Nordsüdbahn, after which they were confined to workmen's services as they were too wide and the motor coaches too long to be used in the tunnel sections. Five half trains had to be scrapped after war damage and the remainder saw little use for some years after the war ended. However, eight half trains were repaired in the 1950s and placed in service on the northern part of the Ring. In 1956/57 these trains were modernised and the motor coaches were both technically and in appearance rebuilt to resemble the Stadtbahn class. They became superfluous after 1961 and were taken out of passenger service the following year. A total of 15 motor coaches were rebuilt as U-Bahn trains in 1967–68, while two motors and two trailers were reformed as a works train for Friedrichsfelde workshops. Several other trailers survived in departmental stock and two of these have now been obtained by the S-Bahn Museum Group for preservation. The remaining half of an unrebuilt motor coach, used as a store at Schöneweide workshops from June 1943, has now been acquired by the S-Bahn Museum group.

The Oranienburg Class of 1925 (Later Class 168)

For the opening of services to Oranienburg and Velten, 50 quarter trains were ordered. Complaints about the poor riding qualities of the Bernau trains led DRG to decide to build only bogie coaches, and these trains were made up of motor coaches and driving trailers. To improve acceleration, all axles on the motor coaches were powered and, at 44.5 tonnes, were somewhat lighter than their predecessors. Double-width doors replaced the single-leaf doors of the previous class and in every respect these trains set the standard for all S-Bahn rolling stock built up to 1939. In 1936, some of the driving trailers had their driving controls removed and after that year, some sets were used on the Ring.

The class suffered heavy losses during the war, in particular during an air raid on Westend depot, and only 19 two-car sets remained in passenger service after 1945, all in West Berlin. These trains also became redundant after 1961 and all remaining sets were rebuilt as U-Bahn trains between then and 1964.

One Oranienburg motor coach has been given to the S-Bahn Museum Group. *Historische S-Bahn e.V.*

The Stadtbahn Class of 1928 (Later Class 165)

This class must rank as one of the most outstanding designs of electric trains of all time. First introduced in 1928, a large number are still in service in 1996, having survived dictatorship, war, the division of Berlin, and the subsequent reunification. Whatever the conditions, this class has just kept on running and running. The original design showed rugged and functional, but still attractive, lines and it has not dated. The class is also famous for having introduced to the S-Bahn the familiar red and ochre livery (until 1946 with blue in the second class areas), which has likewise survived all these upheavals and, more recently, attempts by designers in both parts of the city, to have it replaced by something which was thought to have been more modern. The order for this class, of 638 two-coach sets, was one of the largest single orders ever placed in German railway history. The history of such a large and long-lived class is inevitably complicated and only a brief outline can thus be given here.

While the design of the Oranienburg class had generally proved satisfactory, these had been built for essentially suburban services with fairly wide headways. The new class would operate for part of the time on what was an urban metro and the design had thus to be equally suitable for urban and suburban conditions. As before, the motor coaches were powered on each axle but to improve acceleration, they were considerably lighter, being constructed of silicon steel. Two half-trains of the first batch were constructed of even lighter metal, but this proved to be liable to corrosion and was not repeated.

A two-car preserved set of the Stadtbahn class, seen at the 'temporary' platform at Bornholmer Strasse on the former 'east' section. In original condition, second class accommodation was then identified by the blue-painted section above waist level, at its rear. *Historische S-Bahn e.V.*

45

To provide adequate circulating space and reduce station dwell times, the partitions at the doors were set back slightly on the first batch but this reduced the seating capacity and, after complaints from passengers, second and subsequent batches had the partitions immediately behind the doors. Extra seating was also provided by eliminating doors in internal partitions. Almost all control trailers were composites, except for a few built to work on the northern part of the Ring. This class was the first to have automatic closing of the doors by the guard, but opening remained and remains manual, allowing young Berliners to display their machismo by alighting well before the train has come to a stop! Internal lighting was also greatly improved by the provision of two rows of lamps over the seats in place of one row in the centre of the ceiling.

The two prototypes were half-trains built by Waggonfabrik Waggon-und Maschinen-bau (Görlitz) and Orenstein and Koppel, and these were delivered early in 1928. Series production began in the summer of 1928 and continued until 1931. The trains were built by six manufacturers but to identical designs. Electrical equipment, by Siemens or AEG, was installed in the then newly-completed workshops at Schöneweide. It had been expected that there would be a need to operate a considerable number of two-coach trains in off-peak periods, but the growth of traffic soon put a stop to this idea and almost all of the trailers delivered in 1930 and 1931 lacked control equipment. Most of the control trailers lost this immediately after 1945.

Such a large class was bound to suffer greatly from war damage and this was compounded by the removal of many vehicles as war reparations to Poland and the USSR where, fitted with pantographs for overhead current collection, they ran on suburban services, although some returned to Berlin in 1952. A total of 80 quarter trains ran in Poland (Danzig – Neufahrwasser and Zoppof – Gdingen – Kiehlau – Neustadt) and 156 quarter trains in the USSR (Tallinn – Pasküll and Moskwa – Domodedovo), which were taken from all of the classes available. Between 1957 and 1972, four quarter trains were operated in the Federal Republic of Germany between München and Grünwald and Rosenheim to Kufstein.

A 'Passviertelzüg' formed in the middle of a train operating on the Stadtbahn in 1986, which retained the single headlight and twin tail lamps at roof level, with 275.737 illustrated.
Brian Patton

Around two-thirds of the class remained available for service in Berlin but many of them were in poor condition. To provide spares for damaged vehicles, some coaches lost all their seats on one side and some motor coaches ran for a time as trailers. Not until the end of the 1950s were all the surviving members of the class once again in reasonable condition. During the course of repair, many coaches received fluorescent lighting and wooden doors were replaced by metal.

Above On conversion to one-person-operation, the Stadtbahn class lost the roof-level tail lamps and gained twin headlamps. This train at Lichtenberg on line S7 shows the livery that was applied from the early post-war period – red and ochre. *John Laker*

Centre Interior of class 475 stock, still with wooden seating and tungsten lighting. This view looks towards the trailing end of the car which has a central window with viewing into the adjacent car. *Brian Patton*

Left Flourescent lighting has been fitted to this class 475, seen facing the driving cab. *Nick Agnew*

From 1965 onwards, many of the class were rebuilt for one-person operation. This involved the fitting of a radio, for despatch from stations, and an additional safety control apparatus. The driver's cab had to be enlarged to accommodate this, at the expense of four seats. Outwardly, the most visible sign of rebuilding was the replacement of the single headlamp by twin lights and the removal of the signal lamps from the roof top corners. The internal lighting was also changed from dc to ac.

About two-thirds of the surviving members of the class were thus converted. To speed up the programme, others received only the necessary control wiring modifications and could then be operated only in the middle of a train. Known as 'Passviertelzüge' they retained the single headlight and could thus easily be distinguished. Some of these later part-modified cars received a full rebuild by DR and, later still, some were rebuilt under BVG auspices. In 1970 the class became known as 275.0–8.

Many of the class were further rebuilt from 1979 onwards. The semi-automatic Scharfenberg coupling was given an electric coupling which, in theory, allowed the class to run in multiple with later classes. In practice, this was hardly ever done, as the operating characteristics of the different classes varied too much to make this practicable. A two-piece driver's windscreen replaced the familiar three windows and the interiors were also modernised, the walls being covered in a light green formica-type panelling and the seats upholstered in dark blue, though some trains had earlier received this feature. There was further reclassification to 276.1–5. The last six trains to be modernised, in 1987, were fitted with multiple-step KE brakes and 73 previously modernised two-coach sets were subsequently given this feature, forming a separate sub-class (276.) which could not be operated with non-modified sets.

Facing page, top When the BVG took over West Berlin S-Bahn services in 1984, its trains were subsequently modernised and repainted in red and yellow livery, as seen on this ex-works set at Bellevue. At this time, west and east were still firmly divided and this train is bound for the then terminus and border crossing station at Friedrichstrasse. *Bob Greenaway*

Facing page, bottom From 1987, after some experiments, a new livery was adopted for S-Bahn trains in East Berlin, known as Bordeaux red and ivory. A four-car train of class 475 stock arrives at Storkower Strasse on a short working of line S10 to Blankenburg. *Brian Hardy*

Left Coupling up between class 475 stock with a motor coach in 1987 'east' livery (left) coupled to a trailer in the red and ochre early post-war livery. *Nick Agnew*

When the lines in West Berlin were handed over to the BVG for operation in 1984, 119 motor and 117 trailer coaches of this class were included in the agreement. In general, these were in run-down condition and retained wooden seats, DR having learnt that passengers in the west were inclined to vent their feelings in vandalism to the seats. Between mid-1984 and January 1987, a total of 95 two-coach sets were renovated at the workshops of Waggon-Union in West Berlin, receiving in the process upholstered seats in maroon, to standard DB design. Twelve of the 20 Passviertel trains were also included in this programme and were fitted for one-person operation at the same time – BVG often operated short trains and these gave added flexibility.

A total of 82 coaches of this class were also converted to U-Bahn trains of type E3 and more would have been so treated had not BVB been able to buy a large number of redundant trains from BVG in time for the extension of U-Bahn line U5 in 1989. All these conversions, however, have now been withdrawn from service.

The trains of the original design which are still in service, known since 1992 as class 475/875, are unlikely to last much longer and will be replaced in 1996/97 by new class 481 stock. However, according to current planning in Berlin, the rebuilt sets, now class 476.0/876 and class 476.3–4/876, should run until around 1999 and indeed should outlast the rebuilds of later pre-war classes. By that date, some will have been in service for some 72 years and the Stadtbahn class will rank alongside the Sprague stock of the Paris Métro as one of the classic designs of electric rolling stock of the 20th century.

The Wannseebahn Class of 1932 (Later Class 165.8)

For the opening of electric service on the Wannseebahn, additional trains were required. Following trials with two prototype quarter-trains, 49 two-coach sets were ordered from no fewer than five separate manufacturers and these entered service in 1933. Externally they resembled very closely the previous design, although the side panels were carried further down, giving a smoother effect to the bodywork. Electrically, however, they differed considerably, since they had all-electric, rather than electro-pneumatic equipment, and passengers also enjoyed the luxury of underfloor heating. Until 1961, they remained on the service for which they were built, including the operation of the 'Banker's Express', but from 1939 also working through the Nordsüdbahn to Oranienburg. One train was caught in the flooding of the tunnel in 1945 and another may have been sent abroad as reparations. A total of 36 sets survived and these, with the exception of one trailer, which later passed to the BVG, were removed to the eastern network after 1961 and allocated to Grünau depot, those with upholstered seats going first.

A few sets were rebuilt for one-person operation after 1968, but most remained as 'Passviertel'. However, after 1979, some 23 sets and one spare motor coach were rebuilt in the same manner as the Stadtbahn class, from which they were almost indistinguishable and with which they could work in multiple. They were now classified 275.9 From the renumbering of 1992, they were included with that class. Two sets and two other spare trailers were rebuilt as U-Bahn trains and in 1993 two sets and one spare motor coach still remained in service as one-person trains as altered in 1968. One of the prototype motor coaches has gone to the S-Bahn Museum Group for preservation.

The prototype sets for the electrification of the Wannseebahn differed from the previous Stadtbahn class, in having rectangular cab windows. This was not perpetuated on the production trains and thus these remained unique. This set, with motor coach 275.959 leading, is now in Hundekehle depot. *Historische S-Bahn e.V.*

The Banker and Olympia Classes of 1934 & 1936 (Later Classes 125 & 126)

The Wannseebahn class, with a maximum speed of 80 km/hr may perhaps have had some difficulty keeping up with main line trains on the stretch of line between Potsdamer Bahnhof and Zehlendorf when working the 'Banker's Expresses'. In 1935, DR placed on this service a prototype train of a new design, with a top speed of 120 km/hr and a redesigned and very handsome front end, with a raked profile and three equal-height windows in the driving cab. The four two-coach sets which made up the train differed slightly from each other in lighting and ventilation. The gap between the coaches was slightly reduced and the extra space used to give more room internally, while still keeping the same overall length. The first motor coach from this train, which was not altered externally during its life, has now been preserved by the Museum of Transport and Technology in Berlin.

This was followed in 1936 by a further 44 two-coach sets to the same design, of which six had capability of 120 km/hr and two could reach 140 km/hr, while the remainder, intended to strengthen operation on the route serving the Olympic Games, had the usual 80 km/hr maximum. Outwardly, the only distinguishing mark of the faster trains was a series of streamline strips below the windows. The bogie wheelbase was increased from 2.5m to 2.6m but it was found that this did not provide any noticeable improvement in riding and later trains reverted to the standard length. A further train for 120 km/hr was placed in service in 1938, being built to the then current design but reverted to the 2.5m bogies.

Apart from those kept for preservation, what became the class 277 is now a memory on the S-Bahn, all having been either rebuilt (1974–1982) or withdrawn in 1991. In Bordeaux red and ivory livery, this train pauses at Storkower Strasse. *Historische S-Bahn e.V.*

The 1937/40 Class (Later Class 167)

To cope with the continued increase in traffic and the further increase expected when the Nordsüdbahn was completed, DRG ordered in 1937 a further 80 two-coach trains. Externally these were very similar to the previous class, the only obvious difference being the omission of a separate door for the driver, but the sets were fitted with fully automatic Scharfenberg couplings, in which the electrical part was covered by a cowling known to railwaymen as a 'Klavier' (piano) and this facility prevented working in multiple with any previous design. Auxiliary electrical equipment was fed from a battery and was thus independent of the traction current.

Delivery began in 1938 and, probably in 1939, the order was increased to 211 sets. Because of the outbreak of war, delivery was extended and the last set did not enter traffic until January 1941. One of these sets was the 1,000th two-coach set to be built for the Berlin S-Bahn. The level of wartime traffic led to yet another order for 80 sets in 1941 – delivery continued throughout the war but the order was not fully completed in 1945 and at least six sets were outstanding when hostilities ended. War losses were considerable and 20 sets were sent off to Danzig in 1945, leaving 183 (some sources give 180) in service in Berlin. Several trailers were completed on existing underframes in the 1950s and paired with motor coaches which had been running as trailers but which now had re-acquired motors.

Although intended to work on the Nordsüdbahn, the class was used on all sections after 1945. However, the first shuttle train to work in between Anhalter Bahnhof and Friedrichstrasse in 1946 was made up of two sets from this class. Due to the lack of spare parts, some motor coaches were converted from all-electric to electro-pneumatic operation in post-war years. From 1963 onwards, many of this class were modernised internally, with the installation of upholstered seating and fluorescent lighting, and from the following year conversion to one-person operation began.

Still in early post-war livery, this class 276 train is seen arriving at Friedrichshagen, now line S3, on 22 May 1986. *Bob Greenaway*

Rebuilds from the Bankier and Olympia classes into what is now class 477 were undertaken between 1974 and 1982. In the latest livery, an eight-coach train stands at Bernau on line S8 on 29 June 1993. *Steve Williams*

A class 477 train approaches Warschauer Strasse heading for Friedrichshagen on line S3. In the background can be seen the overall roof of Hauptbahnhof main line station and the television tower at Alexanderplatz. *Nick Agnew*

A second more drastic modernisation of almost all the sets of this and the two preceding classes, by now known as class 277, was undertaken between 1974 and 1982, when these were given new bogies, a new two-piece windscreen and a revised seating arrangement. Although quite similar in appearance in modified form to the modified 476 type, the modernisation of these trains did have visible cosmetic differences to the discerning expert in that the cab ends retained a very slight rake (whereas the others are upright and flat), the upright gap between the two cab windows was narrower, and the lower bodyline over the coupler was not raised quite so high. However, a total of 15 sets were not modernised and were withdrawn in 1991, leaving 166 motor coaches and 165 trailers, now known as classes 477/877 in service.

Above Two class 477 trains stand side-by-side at Ostkreuz on 4 July 1995, the one on the right having been painted into all-over-advert livery in May 1995. *Brian Hardy*

Below What is now the class 476 stock was rebuilt from the Stadtbahn class between 1980 and 1989. They are similar to the previous class 477 rebuilds but lack the slightly raked front as seen (left) at Potsdam Stadt with a class 477 (right) on 29 June 1993. *Steve Williams*

A four-car class 476 train pauses at the temporary Bornholmer Strasse station on 1 July 1994. Note the work being undertaken (left) which will ultimately restore all connections between the former 'west' and 'east' systems. *Brian Hardy*

From 1995 the through Oranienburg–Wannsee trains on S1 have been lengthened from six to eight cars and some have been formed of class 476 stock, further reducing the numbers of class 475 trains in service. This train departs Rathaus Steglitz for Oranienburg in July 1995. *Brian Hardy*

Above Contrast in livery styles on class 476 stock at Westkreuz in June 1994. *Brian Hardy*

Left The class 476 and 477 interiors are quite similar and contrast with the 475 stock in having upholstered seats, fluorescent lighting and audio-visual door-close signals. *Jeanne Hardy*

The Peenemünder Class of 1941

This was the only class to operate on the S-Bahn which was originally built for service elsewhere. A branch line, electrified at 1,100V dc on the overhead system was built to serve the weapons establishment at Peenemünde in 1941 and to operate on it 16 two-coach sets, made up of motor coaches and control trailers and based on the current design for S-Bahn rolling stock, were built. After hostilities ended the 18 surviving coaches were taken to Berlin, in some cases via the USSR, and were rebuilt for third-rail operation, with equipment from war-damaged members of the Stadtbahn class. They were then classified ET/ES 167. Seven sets were again rebuilt with control trailers in 1965 and reclassified ET/ES 166 and were used as two-coach trains on selected lines in off-peak periods. Five sets were modernised in the same manner as the previous design between 1978 and 1980 and one motor was converted to class E3 U-Bahn in 1990, leaving eight sets in service in 1996, numbered as part of class 477/877. One set has been presented to the S-Bahn Museum Group for preservation, while another non-modernised set has, until recently, served as a café at Falkensee station, once having been part of the S-Bahn network.

Left A Peenemünder car before conversion.

Below The Peenemünder conversions to what became the 477 class virtually identical to their counterparts but formed DMSO-DTSO. *Brian Hardy*

The ET 170 Class of 1959

In 1955 DR began planning the construction of a new design of S-Bahn train and initially proposed a nine-coach formation, which would consist of three three-coach sets, each capable of independent operation. It was thought that this would permit more flexibility of operation. To keep the weight of such a train within existing limits, it was decided to adopt articulation with a "Jacobs bogie" between each coach. Closer consideration of the plans showed that such a train would still be too heavy, not least because of the weight of the Jacobs bogies and it was then decided to revert to the standard eight-coach length, but to retain articulation.

The prototype train was shown at the Leipzig Fair of 1959. Unfortunately, all former ideas of good design had been cast aside and the new train had a bulbous and heavy appearance, quite out of keeping with the pre-war sets. After the Fair, it was taken to Berlin and displayed to the public outside the Opera on Unter den Linden.

The train was made up of two four-coach sets, each pair of coaches being articulated together – driving cabs were fitted only at the outer ends of each half-train. A break with tradition was provided by the colour scheme of light blue and off-white. Connecting doors were fitted within each half-train to allow a better distribution of passengers. All end bogies were motored. More powerful motors were fitted to give a top speed of 90 km/hr and there was a reversion to electro-pneumatic control equipment of the type used on the Stadtbahn class. The complete train was 8-metres longer overall than pre-war designs and this allowed more room in the cab and vestibules. A public address system and fluorescent lighting were fitted and pressure ventilation replaced the opening windows of pre-war designs.

In service, apart from its improved riding qualities, the train performed as badly as it looked. The on-board electrical supply was unreliable and ventilation and heating each caused complaints, and there were problems with the brakes and the control equipment, which gave jerky acceleration. The train was shedded at Erkner and was used in service to Friedrichstrasse, but had long periods out of service due to mechanical failure. The first half-train did not run after 1963 and was scrapped ten years later. The second half-train was repainted in traditional colours around 1965 and fitted for one-person-operation. It seemed to perform more regularly but was finally withdrawn in 1972 and scrapped two years later.

The train probably failed due to the number and complexity of new features incorporated in it, although DR deserved credit for trying to improve conditions for its passengers. The surplus of trains after the Wall went up in 1961 made it unnecessary to persevere with such experiments and DR turned to modernisation rather than the replacement of existing trains to keep its system running.

The class ET170 in orginal blue livery seen in the sidings of Schöneweide workshops. This prototype was deemed unsuccessful and had a rather short life, although four cars did survive long enough to be repainted in traditional colours. *Historische S-Bahn e.V.*

The 270 Class of 1980 (Later Class 485/885)

While the rebuilding policy was successful in the short term, it became clear by the mid-1970s that orders for new trains could not indefinitely be postponed. The Stadtbahn stock was now approaching its 50th birthday and there was no longer any surplus stock which could be used to serve the planned extensions.

At the Leipzig Fair of 1980 a prototype half-train of a new design was displayed to the public for the first time. In construction, this train reverted to the well-tried form of two two-coach sets, each made up of a driving motor close-coupled to a trailer. The aluminium bodies were of integral construction, considerably lighter than those of existing trains. The basic layout remained as before but the new train had externally-hung sliding doors and a smartly raked two-piece windscreen. It also introduced another new livery of light maroon and ivory. The driving cab had been carefully planned and was somewhat larger than in former designs. An eight-coach train was in fact three metres longer than a pre-war train, but this extra length did not require any alterations to be made to track or stations. Mechanically, the new trains used chopper control (already tried on two Stadtbahn trains in 1969 and 1974–76) to give smooth acceleration and braking, and the brakes could regenerate current back into the conductor rail, provided another train was then drawing current in the same section. If not, resistances dissipated the energy. A top speed of 90 km/hr could be attained.

After the delivery of a second half-train, line trials began, although some periods were spent in the workshops. The train entered regular service on 5 September 1983. Clearly, DR was anxious to avoid a repetition of the troubles of the 1959 stock.

Due to the pressure of export orders at the manufacturers, series production did not begin until 1987, when eight quarter-trains of the "null" (pre-production) series were placed in service. Internally there were few changes in the arrangement of the lighting and externally the main difference from the prototype was the fitting of square rather than circular headlamps and a slight rearrangement in the front cab windows. A more striking change was the livery carried by one of the new trains, this being painted in a most attractive colour scheme of bright ruby red and anthracite black. This colour scheme became standard for the production series. A more compact form of chopper control was used and more powerful motors – 150kW instead of 125kW – were fitted.

East Berlin prototype 270.003 in Bordeaux red and ivory livery, seen in service at Treptower Park. This station is served by S-Bahn lines S6, S8, S9 and S10. *Historische S-Bahn e.V.*

What was the class 270 for service in East Berlin is now the class 485 (motors) and 885 (trailers) and was delivered in four separate batches from 1987. The initial trains were delivered in Bordeaux red and ivory livery, as seen on 485/885.010. *Historische S-Bahn e.V.*

Since 1990, a total of 166 two-coach sets of what is now class 485/885 have entered service and the class may be seen over most sections of the re-unified S-Bahn system, although rarely, if at all, on the Nordsüdbahn. Delivery was in four distinct batches, with slight variations in the internal layout and originally, only trains of the first two and of the last two series could work together. However, in 1994, trains of the second batch were adapted to allow them to be worked with those of the third and fourth series.

Not surprisingly, the prototype sets could not work in multiple with the production batch and a two-coach set from the prototype was withdrawn as early as August 1986, the remainder of this train following at the end of June 1989. Three of its quarter trains were scrapped in the summer of 1992, but the first was acquired by the S-Bahn Museum Group for preservation. This early withdrawal did not denote that the train was unsuccessful in operation – quite the contrary in fact. Energy saving of the order of 35% over a conventional train amply justified the experiment of chopper control. It was simply the impossibility of working with the production batch and the high cost of rebuilding to enable this to be done that spelled the end for this small sub-class.

The majority of the class 485/885 sets were, however, painted in red and anthracite (dark grey) livery and those in the earlier colours were repainted to conform. With reunification, the class now works in what was east and west Berlin and can be found in service on lines S45, S46, S8 and S9. Here, a train on S8 departs Storkower Strasse for Grünau while a train of class 477 stock calls in the opposite direction, on 30 June 1994. *Brian Hardy*

Interior of class 485/885. *Brian Hardy*

The Class 480

The rolling stock inherited by the BVG in 1984 was in a generally poor condition and was in any case insufficient for the planned expansion of services. In the summer of that year therefore, BVG formed an association with AEG, Siemens and Waggon Union to develop a prototype train for use on its lines. Very fortunately, the government of West Berlin insisted that any such prototype should be capable of operation over the whole S-Bahn system. The prototype cost DEM 12-million, half of which was borne by the Bundesministerium für Forschung und Technologie (Federal Ministry for Research and Technology) and the remainder was carried equally by West Berlin and the suppliers.

The train that finally emerged from Waggon Union's workshops on 22 October 1986 was totally unlike any that had run on the S-Bahn until then. It was made up of four two-coach sets, but for the first time every coach was motored and there was a driver's cab at each end of each set. At that time, BVG often operated short trains and this provision was intended to give flexibility and the option of running two-coach trains. Moreover, two of the sets were painted in contrasting shades of light and dark blue, the former being known officially as crystal blue. On the night of the presentation to the media, one of the local television channels devoted a programme to the new trains and viewers were invited to telephone their comments about the liveries. The TV station's switchboard was jammed, but over 18,000 callers did get through and recorded a majority of 55% for the traditional colours, much to the discomfort and embarrassment of BVG officers and the designer who were taking part in the programme!

Technically, the new train was of advanced design. It was slightly longer than previous classes but also slightly lighter, despite every coach being a motor coach. Each axle was powered by an asynchronous, three-phase motor of 90kW, giving a top speed of 100 km/hr and a very good rate of acceleration of $1m/s^2$. Chopper control was fitted and there was an on-board computer system for diagnosis of faults. The leading motor coaches were numbered 480.0xx and those without a main controller 480.5xx.

The BVG in West Berlin received prototype trains in 1986, which differed greatly in almost all respects from other stocks. They had far more technical innovations than their 485/885 East Berlin counterparts. Two were painted in crystal blue, but have now been repainted in the standard livery. Two two-coach sets approach Humboldthain on line S2 on 6 September 1992. *Alan Blake*

The 480 class comprised two batches, the first ordered by BVG, the second by DR. They can be found in service on lines S1, S2, S25 and S3. A six-car formation approaches Schöneberg on line S1 on 26 June 1994. *Brian Hardy*

The coupling between units of class 480 stock. The set (left) is one of the four prototypes, the set (right) being one of those financed by the European Union as indicated by the flag above the BVG logo. *Nick Agnew*

For the first time since the Oranienburg class, there were only three double doors per side of each coach, but these were somewhat wider than on existing stock and, as there was also ample circulating space inside, it was found that this arrangement allowed station stops to be kept at their existing times. The doors could be operated by passengers using push-buttons and closure was indicated by both audible and acoustic signals, as on DR. Most of the seats, which were upholstered in a light red material, were arranged transversely and legroom was much more generous than on earlier stocks. A public address system was fitted in each coach. An illuminating line route diagram was also included, but was not perpetuated on the production batches.

The train entered trial service in July 1987 and proved successful, and popular with staff and passengers. However, the crystal blue livery did not grow on Berliners, who continued to say what they thought of it at every opportunity. It was finally agreed that this colour scheme would not be perpetuated. In 1989, one coach was painted white, to test a new house style for BVG, but the operators did not dare let this be seen in public service and it was repainted without entering service.

In 1988 BVG ordered 41 two-coach sets from Waggon Union and these entered traffic between October 1990 and July 1992. Externally the main difference from the prototype was the replacement of the dot matrix destination indicator by the traditional roller blind. Internally, there was a rearrangement of the baggage area and vertical handrails were provided. To assist passengers with disabilities, a small ramp was fitted at the inner end door of each coach, extended at stations to bridge the gap between train and platform. There was also a dot matrix display of the next station and final destination along with an automatic announcement of the next station just after departure of the previous one.

It was planned to order further batches, but by 1992 is was obvious that BVG would not remain the operator of the western S-Bahn and the order for 40 sets was placed by DR. These entered service in 1993/94. They may be distinguished from the BVG batch by a different arrangement of the handrails and by the acoustic doors-close warning signal, which is of the standard DR three-note varying pattern instead of the five monotone bleeps of the BVG.

The class 480 sets can be found in service, alongside older stock, on line S3 (Potsdam Stadt to Erkner) and Nordsüdbahn lines S1, S2 and S25. One unit, however, has been withdrawn – 480.025 was burnt out at Lichtenrade in November 1992 and its partner 480.525 was subsequently scrapped at Schöneweide in the summer of 1995.

A contrasting view of the two new stocks side by side in service, at Warschauer Strasse. On the left is the 'west' class 480 on an S3 service to Potsdam Stadt and on the right an 'east' class 485 on an S9 service to Schönefeld Airport.
Capital Transport

Above Interior of a DR-ordered class 480, distinguishable by its lower level handrails.
Capital Transport

Interior of BVG set 480.035, fitted with wooden shaped seats, presumably as an experiment to combat vandalism. The grab rails on the BVG sets extend right up to ceiling level. *Brian Hardy*

The Duo S-Bahn

On either side of the boundary of the former West Berlin, there are still short sections of the former S-Bahn track which have been de-electrified and are still out of use. Examples of this may be found on the lines Spandau–Falkensee and Heiligensee–Henningsdorf. Restoring the former service would require much time and money, and these lines now have a low priority for rebuilding. In addition, the spread of electrification at 15kV, with overhead current collection, has highlighted the problem of operating two systems side by side in a crowded urban area. The provision of separate tracks is costly and in any case there is not always enough room to permit this.

The management of what had by 1993 become AEG Schienenfahrzeuge Hennigsdorf (ASF) suggested that these problems could in part be overcome relatively cheaply by construction of S-Bahn trains with capability of operating on diesel power away from the third rail and went on to put this idea in practice by converting one half-train of class 485/885 into an electro-diesel unit. This involved mounting under the floor of the trailer a six cylinder diesel engine of 280kW coupled to a three-phase generator with the necessary control equipment to allow this to be coupled to the electric motors. Access to this is gained by trap-doors in the floor of the trailer, necessitating some re-arrangement of seats and the fitting of an equipment 'cupboard' against one end wall. This has resulted in a loss of seven seats in the trailer coach. The converted trailer is five tonnes heavier than hitherto. To allow the train to serve stations with platforms lower than those on the present S-Bahn, additional steps have been fitted, operated by the driver – automatic steps could easily be fitted in a production batch.

The converted unit, classified 485/885D and comprising sets 485/885–114 and 485/885–115, went into service between Hennigsdorf and Oranienburg on 30 May 1994, using the third rail between Birkenwerder and the latter. In an accident on 17 June, where the fuel tank was damaged by a pump that had become loose, the train had to be withdrawn for repair. Since then, its appearance in service has been spasmodic and it was withdrawn altogether on 27 May 1995. The train is now stored and faces an uncertain future, being located at Hundekehle since the end of July 1995.

It has to be said that DR was somewhat doubtful about the electro-diesel concept – the rebuilding was carried out by ASF at its own expense, and it remains to be seen if this experiment, or the proposed conversion of another set to dual-voltage operation, will have any long-term prospect with the new S-Bahn administration.

The experimental four-coach class 485/885 'Duo S-Bahn' train, complete with sponsor's branding on the car sides below window level. Following withdrawal in May 1995, the train was observed stored at Friedrichsfelde depot in July 1995. *Historiche S-Bahn e.V.*

The S-Bahn Of The Future – class 481/482

To permit the retirement of all pre-war S-Bahn trains by the end of this century, an order for the first tranche of 100 two-coach sets, was placed with AEG (27 sets) and DWA (73 sets) in July 1994. The new train is to be based on the 480 class but, while all coaches will be motored, the non-driving car (482) will have only one motor bogie, giving six motor bogies per set. Only those at the outer ends of half-trains will have a driving cab, experience having shown that the inner cabs on class 480 sets were seldom used. The trains will be of modular, lightweight, construction to allow both speedy replacement of damaged parts and, later, to allow easy alteration of layout to suit changes in public taste. Again, three-phase drive will be used in conjunction with an on-board computer to govern both acceleration and braking, as well as providing present-time information on the running of the train and diagnosing faults which may occur in service. There will be regenerative braking.

Connections for passengers will be provided within each two-coach set and, for the first time since 1946, two 'classes' will be provided. For the first time also, there will be a full width window behind the driving cab, the aim of which is to increase passenger security – but it will of course provide an interesting view of the 'road' ahead! At present this is available to passengers only on very hot days when some drivers leave their cab door open to improve ventilation. Instead of the present electrical heating (which, on the class 480 stock, has sometimes generated trails of smoke from the top-level vents, giving them the nickname of 'toasters') both heating and cooling will be provided by the circulation of air by a ventilation system mounted in the ceiling. As on class 480, a retractable ramp will be provided for passengers in wheelchairs or with prams or cycles.

The trains will be of the slightly shorter length (36.8 metres per two-coach set) of class 485 and each set will weigh 59 tonnes. Driving motor cars will seat 44 (14 on tip-up seats) and non-driving cars 50, of which 12 will be first class. With standing passengers at 4 per m^2, the total capacity of a quarter train will be 294.

The first ten pre-production sets should be complete by the end of 1996. Meanwhile, the option for a further 400 quarter trains has been converted into a firm order, with delivery likely to run from 1998 to 2004.

When all the new class 481/482 trains are delivered, the remaining classes 475, 476 and 477 – all of 1927–42 vintage – will become a memory.

The S-Bahn's latest stock – a train of class 481/2. *AEG*

S-Bahn Station Design

The vast majority of S-Bahn stations in Berlin comprise platforms of the 'island' type. There are only five side platform stations, which are Buckower Chaussee and Schichauweg (S2), Biesdorf (S5), Ahrensfelde (S7) and Bornholmer Strasse (S8/10). There are, of course, the multi-platform stations on the much busier sections of line and at interchange stations. In addition, there are platforms which have been built as 'islands' but are used as single side platforms because of the 'missing' second track. These are as follows:

Line	Station	Line	Station
S2	Blankenfelde	S5	Hegermühle
S25	Lankwitz	S5	Strausberg Stadt
S25	Alt-Reinickendorf	S8	Röntgental
S25	Karl-Bonhoeffer-Nervenklinik	S10	Mühlenbeck-Mönchmühle
S25	Eichborndamm	S10	Oberspree
S46	Wildau	S10	Spindlersfeld
S5	Neuenhagen	S45, S46, S6, S8, S9, S10 }	Baumschulenweg (northbound only)
S5	Petershagen Nord		

At platform level, the character of the S-Bahn, most often in the suburbs, is portrayed by the brick-built accommodation, mainly for staff purposes. These buildings are distinctive in having decorative tile patterns although recent attention by graffiti vandals has caused some of them to be over-painted. The larger stations in the city centre have been built on a grandiose scale and share them with main line trains, such as Alexanderplatz, Friedrichstrasse and Hauptbahnhof, all of which have impressive overall roofs. But it is the station buildings themselves where architectural merit has been surpassed in many cases.

Looking left, a view of the new platforms under construction at Bornholmer Strasse in June 1994, with, at far left, present lines S1, S2 and (from 1995) S25. *Jeanne Hardy*

The exterior of Nikolassee, serving lines S1, S3 and S7. The building dates back to 1901/02 and was designed by Fritz Bräuning and is in late gothic/renaissance style. It is seen in restored condition on 27 May 1986. *Alan Blake*

Botanischer Garten on line S1 comprises a Prussian art-nouveau building of 1908/09, along with this unique entrance. *Nick Agnew*

Rahnsdorf on line S3 dates back to 1899–1902 and is reminiscent of an historic 'castle', complete with turrets. It is seen on 22 May 1986. *John Laker*

Exterior of Wollankstrasse station building, serving lines S1, S2 and S25. This station was right on the border between 'east' and 'west' and between 1961 and 1989 it was available only to West Berliners. *Capital Transport*

The platforms of S1 and S3/S7 at Nikolassee are totally separate and on a different alignment. Those of the former are illustrated here and show the tiled platform buildings to be found on many S-Bahn suburban stations. *Alan Blake*

Mexikoplatz, formerly Lindenthaler Allee, was built in 1904/05, being designed by Hart and Lesser in an exotic art nouveau design. *Capital Transport*

Feuerbachstrasse on S1 was built in 1932–33 and was designed by Richard Brademann. This, along with some other stations on both the S-Bahn and U-Bahn, were built to similar designs used on the London Underground around the same period. *Nick Agnew*

Platform level at Schöneberg on line S1, before the Ring (at the upper level) was reopened, shows that the escalator leading up to it was left in boarded-up condition. How much of it remained underneath is open to speculation. *Nick Agnew*

Bellevue station on the Stadtbahn dates back to 1878–80 and was designed by Johann Eduard Jacobsthal. This station was restored in 1987 but closed temporarily from October 1994 during the reconstruction of the route between Zoologischer Garten and Hauptbahnhof. *Brian Patton*

Probably the busiest and most interesting station on the S-Bahn system is at Ostkreuz, serving eight lines and with the same number of platforms, spread out in three locations. The lower level has four platforms serving lines S3, S5, S7 and S75, while the 'country' end has a high-level island platform serving lines S8 and S10. *John Laker*

At the west (city) end of Ostkreuz there are two separate high-level platforms, one of which is used by inbound services on lines S6 and S9 (these do not stop at Ostkreuz in the outward direction), while the other platform is now disused, there no longer being a direct service from the city to the eastern part of the Ring. The lower-level island platform in the foreground serves line S3. *John Laker*

A view of Witzleben station on the Ringbahn, taken from the Funkturm (radio tower). Note the two entrances to the station. The next bridge from the left-hand entrance contains U-Bahn line U2, underground but passing over the Ringbahn and adjacent motorway. *Brian Hardy*

The station at Bornholmer Strasse in West Berlin, now serving lines S1, S2 and S25, was of 1935 design by Richard Brademann. It closed on 13 August 1961 because of the Wall. The adjacent tracks of lines S8 and S10 never had a station, but after the 'west' station reopened on 22 December 1990, temporary platforms for S8 and S10 were provided from 5 August 1991. These temporary platforms will be replaced by permanent ones to the left when all the line and track connections are completed – probably around 1999. *Jeanne Hardy*

Potsdamer Platz was the last of the closed S-Bahn underground stations to reopen – on 1 March 1992. It originally comprised two island platforms and the station was designed in 1937–38 by Richard Brademann. At present, only the outer platform faces are in use, the inner two being screened off. This dismal station is as visited in June 1994. *Brian Hardy*

Access, too, to street level at Potsdamer Platz is by temporary stairs and handrails, with temporary wooden flooring. This is the ticket hall area (with very few ticket facilities). Not all station entrances have yet reopened and some still remain in 'abandoned' condition. *Capital Transport*

Unter den Linden underground station, now serving lines S1, S2 and S25, reopened on 1 September 1990 after 29 years of closure. It continues to retain much of its 1935/36 character, being one of many stations designed by Richard Brademann and, like Oranienburger Strasse, has a rather low roof. *Brian Hardy*

Anhalter Bahnhof was also designed by Richard Brademann in 1935–36. It has since been refurbished twice and the last occasion in 1986 involved restoration to original style. *Capital Transport*

Power Supply, Signalling and Control

Power Supply

For the first electrified lines to Bernau and Oranienburg, four substations were built. For the route to Velten, two new substations operating with mercury steam rectifiers of each 1,200kW were created. The current was provided by the BEWAG and was brought to the six substations by railway-owned 30kV cables. With the beginning of the main electrification scheme, DRG signed an agreement with the BEWAG and the EWAG, the two large Berlin current companies, both delivering 50% each of the power needed for the S-Bahn. At both ends of the Stadtbahn, switch gear (Schaltwerke) has been installed, which took electric current as alternating current of 30kV.

In the East, the switch gear Markgrafendamm near Ostkreuz station, took current from the power station Klingenberg, in the West switch gear Halensee took current via cable from the power station West at Charlottenburg.

The railway-owned 30kV alternating current cable network was fed by the two switch gears. In 1928 the four old substations of the northern routes and 44 others were connected to the cable network.

On the Stadtbahn and Ringbahn, each station had a substation provided with two rectifiers. The benefit of this system is that the drop of voltage inside the current rail is very low, because starting trains will pick up the largest amount of current when near the rectifier. The 31 rectifier units of the Stadtbahn and Ringbahn were operated by switch gear at Markgrafendamm, Halensee, Schöneberg and at Böttgerstrasse (near to Gesundbrunnen station).

On the suburban lines, substations with three or four rectifiers were built, each serving a 15 km stretch of line. To reduce a loss of voltage, at the meeting point of the two rectifier areas, so-called couple points (Kuppelstellen) were created.

During the 1930s, new rectifiers with a permanent power of 2,400kW were built, and at the beginning of the 1940s, the Berlin S-Bahn network had 55 rectifier units with a power of 208,000kW, the world's largest such system.

In the 1960s DR started to build more rectifiers to strengthen the current supply and to modernise the rectifiers. Since 1986 electric energy has been received as alternating current at 110kV, and is stepped down in a transformer station near Markgrafendamm to 30kV. More transformer stations are planned near Pankow, Halensee and Schöneberg.

The current rail is of the 'Wannseebahn' type on most lines, with the exception of special current rails inside the Nordsüd tunnel and on bridges. The current rail with its 800V direct current is 1570 mm away from the middle of the track and 135 mm above the edge of the running rail. In most cases the current rail is on the left hand side of the track, with the exception of the stations, where the current rail is always furthest away from the platform. The collector shoe touches the current rail from below. Every 5.5 metres the current rail casing is attached to the sleepers via supporting brackets.

The collector shoes are fixed to both sides of both outer bogies of a two-car set by a wooden or plastic beam. All four are connected by an equalisation lead and it is thus possible to bridge gaps of up to 27 metres in the current rail, such as at crossovers.

Left Current collection by S-Bahn trains and the Wide Profile U-Bahn lines is by third rail with underside contact. The current rail itself has a shroud around its top for protection. *Bob Greenaway*

Right The mechanical trainstop bar, to be found universally around the S-Bahn network – this at the temporary station at Hackescher Markt. *Brian Hardy*

Signalling

The original signals on the Stadtbahn and other lines were manually-operated semaphores with a manual block system. In 1928, in connection with the 'great electrification', DRG introduced the first automatically operated colour light signalling system for what became the S-Bahn lines, and by 1943 this covered about half of the network. It allowed a headway of 90 seconds, compared with 2½ minutes of the manual system. The system is known as Sv signalling (Signalverbindungen) and was totally different from that used on the main line railways.

The lines are divided into separate block sections, each protected by a signal, which is controlled from the next block signal ahead. As soon as the first axle of a train has passed a signal, it goes to red and is cleared only when the last axle of the train has passed the next signal.

The colour aspects are controlled by relay-operated glass diaphragms. Both the main and the distant signals are indicated by three colour lights, those on the left of the Sv signal being the main signal, showing if the section ahead is clear and the speed at which it may be traversed, while the indications on the right are the distant signals for the next main signal ahead. Indications are as follows:

Signal	Lights of signal	Meaning of signal
Sv 1	green-green	full speed – expect full speed
Sv 2	green-yellow	full speed – expect stop
Sv 3	green-green yellow	full speed – expect slow speed
Sv 4	green-green yellow	slow speed – expect full speed
Sv 5	green-green yellow-yellow	slow speed – expect slow speed
Sv 6	green-yellow yellow	slow speed – expect stop
Sv 0	yellow-yellow	stop – drive on sight
Hp 0	red	stop

Both fully automatic and semi-automatic Sv signals are in use. The former are used as block signals and as entry or starter signals at stations where there are no points. On these, the normal aspect is Sv 1. Semi-automatic signals are used at stations where there are several tracks in the same direction and to cover branch junctions and sidings. The normal aspect for these is Hp 0. Sv signals and automatic operation of such can be used only on double-track lines.

When the main lines around Berlin were electrified by DR in the 1980s, all Sv signals on S-Bahn lines running near main lines were replaced by common user colour light main signals (Lichthauptsignale, also referred to as HL signals). Although the Sv signals could have been adapted to work alongside the new system, their age and poor condition meant that their replacement was a more economic proposition. Together with the newly introduced AB 70 S automatic block system, the HL signals allowed a much higher frequency of service than could be obtained with the Sv signals. The outer radial routes of the network also received new HL signal equipment in these years, along with new signal boxes. Semaphore signals are no longer used on the S-Bahn.

The following block systems are now in use on the S-Bahn system:

Panel block or station block – Zeuthen–Königs Wusterhausen, Hoppegarten–Fredersdorf, Grünauer Kreuz–Altglienicke, Oranienburg–Lehnitz and Lichtenrade–Blankenfelde.

Relay block – Petershagen Nord–Strausberg Nord, Lehnitz–Birkenwerder, Buch–Schönhauser Allee, Arkenberge–Karower Kreuz, Springpfuhl–Wartenberg, Karlshorst–Erkner, Schöneweide–Spindlersfeld, Schöneweide–Grünauer Kreuz, Altglienicke–Flughafen Berlin-Schönefeld, Buch–Bernau, Schönfleiss–Arkenberge and Wannsee–Potsdam.

Axle counting block – Birkenwerder–Schönholz, Birkenwerder–Schönfleiss, Grossgörschenstrasse–Wannsee, Westkreuz–Wannsee, and Priesterweg–Lichtenrade.

Automatic block – Schönhauser Allee–Schöneweide, Grünauer Kreuz–Eichwalde, Friedrichstrasse–Hoppegarten, Biesdorfer Kreuz–Ahrensfelde and Hauptbahnhof–Karlshorst.

On the ex-BVG routes of the S-Bahn, colour light signals of both DR and DB types are in use. The last Sv signals are also to be found on these lines, for example, between Anhalter Bahnhof and Grossgörschenstrasse. Before November 1989, it had been planned to replace the antiquated signalling on the western network with the electronic EZS 800 system developed by Siemens, but after reunification, DB and DR jointly decided against this hitherto untried system in favour of the electronic system (ESTW) which had already been in use for some years on DB. In the early summer of 1993, two such boxes, at Wannsee and Westkreuz, were brought into operation, their commissioning being linked to the electrification of the main line inwards from Griebnizsee to Zoologischer Garten.

These elektronische Stellwerke (referred to as ETSW) operate in conjunction with the newly introduced combination signals (Kombinationsignale, or Ks signals) first between Potsdam and Lehrter Stadtbahnhof, then on the Ring between Westend and Köllnische Heide, and later between Papestrasse and Licherfelde Ost. Ks signals separate the information controlling the running of trains from that concerning speed. The former is shown by a single point of light (red, yellow, green or flashing green) while the latter is shown by white or yellow figures which indicate the speed permissible in the block sections behind and immediately ahead of the signal. All sections which are operated under the ESTW system will in future be fitted with Ks signals and they will also be fitted for reversible operation.

Along with the Sv signals, a train stop system was introduced on the S-Bahn lines from the end of the 1920s. This consists of two main parts – (1) a reversible arm projecting from the right hand side of the front bogie of every motor and control trailer (Fahrsperre) and (2) a trackside apparatus (Streckenanschlag), which is a movable barrier. This barrier moves to the side when the signal is at clear, but should a train attempt to pass a signal at danger, the arm on the bogie will come into contact with this barrier and an emergency application of the train's brakes will be made. The system has worked very well and has been retained even on those sections which have the latest equipment, though it may be replaced in future by a system yet to be chosen. Such a system would have to permit a headway of 90 seconds on the busiest sections of line – the Stadtbahn, Nordsüdbahn and the Ring, along with some outer sections and one of at least two minutes on other sections.

The outer suburban trains of the main line railway share the same platform as those of the S-Bahn at such places as Birkenwerder and thus 3rd rail and overhead is provided. A class 475 train arrives on a southbound working on S1 and comprises one of the few sets which contains a driving trailer. *Brian Hardy*

AC and DC Operation on the Berlin S-Bahn Network

If dc and high-voltage ac trains were to be operated on the same network, the electric systems would have to be galvanically separated – if not, the high amperage of the return current from dc motors would overheat an overhead line, to the point where it would begin to burn. Other considerations also play a part and local factors must also be taken into account. If, for example, the return dc current goes direct to earth, as at the boundary between the Polish and German systems at the bridge across the border river at Frankfurt (Oder), there is scarcely any problem. But in a system such as Berlin, with many dc lines parallel to ac main lines, with many substations, it is totally different and a galvanic separation of the two systems is the most economical form of operation.

A disadvantage of the dc system is that it is extremely liable to corrode surrounding metal objects – 1 amp of d.c. current can, for example, eat through 9.1 kg of iron in a year. As a result, the running rails which are used for current return must be insulated as closely as possible to prevent leakage to earth. In the a.c. system, with its high voltage, all metal parts are directly earthed and there is a risk that the overhead line may rupture, while there is practically no risk of breakage of the third rail in dc operation. The ac system has good earthing properties, which are in themselves a protection. On this ground also, a strict galvanic separation of the two systems is necessary.

In Berlin, before main line electrification, it was universal practice to use parallel main lines for the current return of the dc S-Bahn, but this is ruled out in parallel operation of ac and dc electrics. The necessity for galvanic separation was one of the main reasons for the delay in extending main line electrification to Berlin in 1983/84, when the western part of the Outer Ring was electrified. With further main line electrification there are increased problems where trains of both systems have to share tracks or cross each other, as at Birkenwerder (lines S1 and S10) and Erkner (S3). To find a solution, we have to look at the history of lines in Hamburg.

After the trials of a.c. operation on the Spindlersfeld branch in Berlin, it was decided to electrify the Hamburg–Blankenese–Ohlsdorf line at 6,300V/25Hz and this went into operation on 1 October 1907. On 12 March 1923, the service was extended to Poppen-büttel. In 1937, the law creating Greater Hamburg foresaw an expansion of S-Bahn operation, including a section in tunnel, and to allow for the use of tunnels of smaller profile, it was decided to use dc current with third rail collection. It was anticipated that there would be only a short overlap between ac and dc operation, but in fact, because of the war, this overlap lasted for 15 years – from 22 April 1940 until 22 May 1955. The ac lines already had good insulation to prevent leakage to earth, probably to a greater extent than would be considered necessary today, and electrically the system was isolated, having its own power station in Altona and a reserve station in Barmbek. It was therefore unnecessary to provide a transformer with galvanic separation. However, when main line electrification reached Hamburg ten years after the end of this operation, it was necessary to reconsider the question. Platform 4 at Altona, for example, had to be used by trains of both systems. The method adopted was to use a system, controlled from the signal box via the entry points, which allowed either ac or dc current to be supplied, the other being cut off. This system lasted until the beginning of the building of the Hamburg City Line in 1977/78.

There was no problem at the first station in Berlin – Flughafen Berlin-Schönefeld – to be served by both systems, as the tracks of each system were physically well separated and the return current of the S-Bahn was led by cables, as well as by its own tracks, back to the substation. However, east of the station, there was a track connection but this was fitted with a double isolation separation (DZA – Doppelte Zweischienige Abtrennung). This consisted of two successive isolation stretches, 3.5 metres apart and this also served to demarcate the operational areas of two signal boxes. This system was later extended to all stations where the two systems had a track connection.

At Birkenwerder, however, the outer suburban trains had to use the S-Bahn platforms and there was no room to build separate platforms for future ac operation. In any case, direct interchange between the two types of trains was required. This raised the question of separating or isolating the ac lines from return current from the dc lines – in other words, the electrical separation of this section from the rest of the ac network. This was achieved by installing two DZA in the southern and northern points and these could be traversed by ac trains only with the master controller shut off – i.e. without drawing power. The overhead in the platforms and the S-Bahn sidings are electrically separated by a transformer in Hohen Neuendorf substation and the controller of this can be shut off in emergency. The works for the installation of this system themselves required special protection. In regular operation, the limited power of the transformer requires operation at only 200A, but in practice this is hardly noticeable, as trains are in any case travelling at slow speed. The system came into service on 28 September 1983. A new platform at Birkenwerder for Regional trains is now planned.

Where there was a need for parallel operation over a longer distance, such as on the Outer Ring between Karow West and Schönfleiss, separate tracks were provided and brought into service on 2 September 1984, the main line tracks being energised on 15 December of the same year. Another S-Bahn station with joint operation was Königs Wusterhausen, where track 3 of platform B could be used by either ac or dc trains, though there was no need to provide for a joint service, and a change of current on the Hamburg model would have sufficed. The points were also fitted with two DZA sections and the main line tracks were connected by underground cables. This section went into service on 16 October 1987 but is no longer operated by S-Bahn trains and thus the special works have since been removed.

Since 1990, Erkner on line S3 had been provided with an example of mixed operation. At peak hours, it is necessary to use platform B, track 4, for S-Bahn trains. This track is also used by terminating outer suburban trains and, at the time the system came into operation, their locomotives had to run round the train, using the track between the platforms – today, push-pull operation has abolished this practice. At platform B, track 4 and track 5 from and to Berlin can only be reached by S-Bahn tracks 11, 12 and 25, and these have both third rail overhead. Mixed operation can therefore be confined to these tracks. Both groups of tracks belong to different control groups and are normally supplied with current by isolating transformers. There are also special measures for current return.

Train Control

As with the U-Bahn, there is no central control point, although with the introduction of ESTW, it will be possible to know the exact position of each train on the entire network. At present, trains entering or leaving service are controlled either by local signal boxes or depots, or by local station staff, to whom drivers have to report before taking over trains in service.

The network is divided into areas of Zugleitung or ZL (train control areas) which are responsible for control within a specific area. These have telephone contact with stations and signal boxes and radio contact with trains.

In addition, since February 1992, there have been regional control, areas. Area 'Ost' (East) is responsible for the lines from Hauptbahnhof to Wartenberg, Ahrensfelde, Strausberg Nord and Erkner, while 'Ring' looks after the sections Westend–Baumschulenweg, Hohen Neuendorf–Spindlersfeld, Bernau–Flughafen Berlin–Schönefeld and Adlershof–Königs Wusterhausen. These are located in the S-Bahn headquarters in Invalidenstrasse. The former BVG control centre Betriebsleitstelle S-Bahn, or BLS, which is situated like that for the U-Bahn in BVG headquarters, has now become the regional control Nord-Süd, being responsible for the sections Oranienburg–Wannsee, Anhalter Bahnhof–Blankenfelde, Tegel–Schönholz and Priesterweg–Lichterfelde Ost.

Co-ordination of these at management level is carried out by Betriebsleitung S-Bahn and Oberzugleitung – train supervision S-Bahn and main line train supervision.

Train Services and Depots

The political upheavals over so many years had a profound effect on train services, especially in West Berlin, as we have already seen. It would be far too time- and space-consuming to detail here the numerous service patterns over the years and this section will deal with the present and only the very recent past. It is true to say that all S-Bahn services are based on a 20-minute operating pattern on all lines on a daily basis, intensified to 10 minutes or diluted to 40 minutes, according to demand and track layout constraints of the line concerned. In city centres, where a number of lines may come together over the same sections of track, (for example S3, S5, S7, S75 and S9 between Warschauer Strasse and Friedrichstrasse), service headways can be as little as 2½ minutes, with eight trains in each 20-minute period.

The present line identification system ('S' letter, followed by a line number) was imported from the S-Bahn networks elsewhere in Germany, which have had it since the mid-1960s.

Once through services had been restored and re-established on the cross-city Stadtbahn through Friedrichstrasse on 2 July 1990, and the section Wannsee – Potsdam Stadt had been re-electrified, services and routes were reorganised as follows:

Line	Between
S1	Oranienburg – Wannsee
S2	Schönholz – Blankenfelde
S3	Potsdam Stadt – Erkner
S5	Charlottenburg – Strausberg Nord
S6	Westkreuz – Königs Wusterhausen
S7	Alexanderplatz – Ahrensfelde
S75	Alexanderplatz – Wartenberg
S8	Bernau – Grünau
S85	Blankenburg – Spindlersfeld
S86	Buch – Warschauer Strasse
S9	Westkreuz – Flughafen Berlin-Schönefeld
S10	Birkenwerder – Schöneweide

The subsequent provision of two passing loops between Wannsee and Potsdam Stadt (at Griebnitzsee and Babelsberg stations) enabled the service to Potsdam Stadt to be doubled to a 10-minute frequency during 1993, achieved by extending line S7 westwards from Alexanderplatz.

The reopening of the south-west section of the Ringbahn in December 1993 saw more radical changes to the S-Bahn services listed above. Two distinct services were provided on the Ringbahn from Westend, both operating every 20 minutes, S45 to Flughafen Berlin-Schönefeld and S46 to Königs Wusterhausen. In consequence of this, S6 became a peak-hours-only service between Warschauer Strasse and Zeuthen and S75 extended west from Alexanderplatz to Westkreuz. Line S10 thus no longer served Schönefeld Airport and was diverted instead to serve the single-track branch to Spindlersfeld, replacing S85 and enabling S86 to be withdrawn. From 24 September 1994, S6 was restored to daily operation with the exception of evenings and weekend early mornings.

A class 477 train in red and cream livery approaches Tempelhof on line S45 on an inner rail Ring service to the present terminus of Westend. *Brian Hardy*

Most services on Ring line S45 are operated by modern class 485/885 stock, but sometimes older types can be seen. A six-car train of type 477 in Bordeaux red and beige livery arrives at Westkreuz on 3 July 1995. In the background can be seen the buildings of Berlin's main exhibition area. *Brian Hardy*

The reopening of the routes to Lichterfelde Ost and Tegel on 28 May 1995 resulted in trains on line S2 being cut back from Waidmannslust (daytime) and Schönholz (all-day, daily) to Nordbahnhof. At the same time, new lines S25 and S26 provided services from Lichterfelde Ost to Tegel and Waidmannslust respectively, the latter being a daytime service only. The shortening of line S2 immediately caused passenger complaints, in that those from Blankenfelde and Lichtenrade no longer had a through service to the northern Berlin suburbs. A further change from 13 July 1995 redressed this problem, by alternate trains on S2 being extended to Waidmannslust and trains on S26 being terminated at Nordbahnhof, these becoming short workings of line S25 from 15 October 1995.

A class 475 at a typical S-Bahn suburban station, Schlachtensee. *Brian Patton*

The Traffic Day and All-night Services

With minor exceptions, services on the S-Bahn start just after 04.00 and finish between 00.30 and just after 01.00. However, at weekends (Friday night/Saturday and Saturday night/Sunday) an all-night service is provided over almost all of the system. The section not covered by such a service is on S10 between Hohen Neuendorf and Blankenburg. Until May 1995, the all-night services were hourly and with the amount of line duplication, not all routes operate for their complete length at night (marked * below) and passengers will often need to change trains.

The reopening of line S25 and its hourly all-night service means that the Nord-Süd-bahn now has a 30-minute service, combined with S1 between Anhalter Bahnhof and Schönholz. In addition, the night service on line S7 is increased to half-hourly on the Stadtbahn between Westkreuz and Lichtenberg. Sections of line operating throughout the night as follows:

Line		Between
S1		Oranienburg – Wannsee
S2	*	Priesterweg – Blankenfelde
S25		Lichterfelde Ost – Tegel
S3	*	Hauptbahnhof – Erkner
S46		Westend – Königs Wusterhausen
S5	*	Lichtenberg – Strausberg Nord
S7		Potsdam Stadt – Ahrensfelde
S75	*	Lichtenberg – Wartenberg
S8/9	*	Bernau – Flughafen Berlin-Schönefeld
S10	*	Schöneweide – Spindlersfeld

Trains Scheduled in Peak Service
Monday to Friday

LINE	Eight-car	Six-car	Four-car	Total Trains	Stock Type(s)
S1	10	8	-	18	475, 476, 480
S2	-	11	-	11	475, 480
S25	-	-	10	10	475, 480
S3	17	-	-	17	477, 480
S45	-	6	} 7	20	477, 485
S46	7	-			
S5	16	-	-	16	476, 477
S6	-	-	4	4	476, 477
S7	} 28	-	-	28	476, 477
S75					
S8	9	6	-	15	476, 477, 485
S9	7	-	-	7	485
S10	-	-	12	12	475, 476

In red and ochre livery, an eight-car train of class 477 stock arrives at Charlottenburg on line S3 on 7 September 1992, heading for Potsdam Stadt. The all-day service to Potsdam is provided by S7, the S3 being a 'daytime busy' service only. On the right, one of the S-Bahn 'reserve' trains can be seen, stored in the eastern siding. *Alan Blake*

The following lists the various locations that are used for train stabling, and from where trains enter service on Mondays to Fridays. The note * indicates that another line's trains also start and stable at that location.

S1:		
Oranienburg	2	*
Birkenwerder	1	*
Anhalter Bahnhof	1	
Zehlendorf	2	
Wannsee	5	*
Gesundbrunnen	1	
Frohnau	3	
Waidmannslust	2	
Nordbahnhof	1	*
Total:	18	

S2:		
Nordbahnhof	2	*
Potsdamer Platz	2	
Papestrasse	1	
Marienfelde	1	
Lichtenrade	3	
Mahlow	1	
Blankenfelde	1	
Total:	11	

S25:		
Tegel	2	
Nordbahnhof	4	*
Lichterfelde Ost	4	
Total:	10	

S3:		
Erkner	7	
Friedrichshagen	1	
Köpenick	2	
Grünau	2	
Hauptbahnhof	1	
Wannsee	3	*
Potsdam Stadt	1	
Total:	17	

S45/46:		
Westend	3	
Bundesplatz	2	
Papestrasse	1	
Hermannstrasse	2	
Königs Wusterhausen	2	
Grünau	2	*
Schöneweide	8	*
Total:	20	

S5:		
Strausberg Nord	2	
Strausberg	1	
Hoppegarten	2	
Mahlsdorf	3	
Lichtenberg	3	*
Charlottenburg	1	*
Grunewald	4	*
Total:	16	

S6:		
Grünau	4	*
Total:	4	

S7/75:		
Potsdam Stadt	2	
Grunewald	4	*
Charlottenburg	1	*
Warschauer Strasse	2	
Lichtenberg	13	*
Ahrensfelde	4	
Wartenberg	2	
Total:	28	

S8:		
Bernau	4	
Buch	1	
Blankenburg	1	*
Greifswalder Strasse	2	*
Ostkreuz	2	
Schöneweide	2	*
Grünau	3	*
Total:	15	

S9:		
Grünau	2	
Flughafen Berlin-Schönefeld	2	
Westkreuz	3	
Total:	7	

S10:		
Oranienburg	4	*
Birkenwerder	2	*
Blankenburg	1	*
Greifswalder Strasse	1	*
Lichtenberg	2	*
Schöneweide	1	*
Spindlersfeld	1	
Total:	12	

The shed at Oranienburg at the northern end of S1 also serves stock on line S10, although it is used only for minor maintenance. South of the depot are open sidings, where a class 476 train is seen (left) and a withdrawn class 277 motor coach (right) on 28 August 1992. *John Laker*

The major maintenance and heavy repair workshops are located at Schöneweide, having been built in 1926–27. The three main maintenance depots, and the lines they serve, are **Friedrichsfelde** (S5, S7, S75 and S10), **Grünau** (S3, S45, S46, S6, S8 and S9) and **Wannsee** (S1, S2, S25 and S3). Friedrichsfelde was built in 1970, but that at Wannsee was built in 1932–33 and was substantially rebuilt after the BVG took over the West Berlin S-Bahn services from January 1984. In addition, there are minor maintenance depots, at **Oranienburg**, **Bernau**, **Erkner** and **Hundekehle** and all, apart from the last named, being in the vicinity of the station of the same name. Hundekehle is located south-west of Grunewald on the Stadtbahn. Although built for steam coaching stock between 1905 and 1910, it was partially rebuilt in 1994, although some of the old sheds still remain.

There was also a minor maintenance depot at **Velten**, which, of 1927 origin, continued to function until September 1983 for the isolated S-Bahn shuttle between there and Hennigsdorf. A surface depot was provided from 1927 at **Nordbahnhof** which closed in 1984 after the BVG took over the S-Bahn services in West Berlin. Plans exist for a new depot to be built here, on a new site east of the present S-Bahn tracks. On the Ringbahn, a depot was built in 1927 at **Papestrasse**. Although the remaining sections of the Ring closed in 1980, the depot remained active until 1992, from when it has been closed for major reconstruction. There was also a depot at **Westend** but this was destroyed in the Second World War and has never been replaced.

The trailing end of a two-coach class 475 train in Wannsee depot, as seen on 27 May 1986, at which time the depot was under reconstruction. *John Laker*

A class 475 set receives attention in Wannsee depot in May 1986 during rebuilding after takeover by the BVG. *Brian Patton*

A line-up of S-Bahn engineering vehicles at Zehlendorf on line S1 on 6 September 1992. *Alan Blake*

Diesel shunting locomotive 5073 in the depot yard at Wannsee. *John Laker*

S-Bahn Fares and Tickets

Not long after the opening of the Stadtbahn, a special fare structure was introduced in 1886. In 1890 this was replaced by a zone tariff and, in turn, on 1 October 1891, this tariff was simplified so that the Stadtbahn and Ringbahn formed only two zones, while reduced fares were made available on all radial lines which had significant suburban traffic. On 1 April 1893, reduced rate season tickets were introduced on these lines. This special tariff was from time to time extended to other lines and destinations, such as to Tegel in 1908 and Velten in 1913. Apart from alterations during the post-1918 period, especially during the time of inflation, this fare structure remained basically unaltered from its inception until 1944. It had, however, become more complicated and in the last pre-war tariff, for example, there were no fewer than 28 different fares on offer and the efficient operation of the system required much time and a large number of booking office and associated staff. The great diversity was also due to transit fares with other forms of public transport.

By the autumn of 1944, under conditions of total war, it had become difficult to maintain this tariff since, in addition to the problems mentioned above, there was also now a severe shortage of card. On 1 October 1944, therefore, was introduced the so-called 'war tariff', which in fact lasted for 47 years without any major change in its structure in the eastern part of the city. The core of the new system was a central area bounded by the Ring, which formed a single zone. Outwards from that were five other zones, the breadth of each being approximately 10 km. For a journey in one or two adjacent zones, passengers paid a fare at price level '1' and each additional zone cost one price level more, with a maximum of eight levels. The total number of fares was reduced from 28 to eight and there were only three reduced rates available, in place of the previous eleven. Second class fares were still available, mainly because there was insufficient labour in workshops to convert second class to third class, and it was thought that if second class areas were still available at third class prices, passengers would seek them out and thus prolong station dwell times. Care was taken to avoid any great increase in fares as a result of these changes, mainly by the introduction of 10-journey tickets. There was no reduction for children over the age of four (under that age they travelled free) but as there were few children left in Berlin by October 1944, this did not matter greatly. The basic fare was 20 Pf and the maximum RM 1.30. The new tariff was successful in every aspect, but was, of course, soon overtaken by the collapse of the S-Bahn service.

When services resumed, from June 1945, only single fares were available. Ten-journey tickets reappeared on 1 April 1946 but with no reduction in price. Second class was also abolished with effect from 1 November 1946 when monthly tickets and scholars' monthly tickets became available. Despite fare increases in all zones of occupied Germany, the S-Bahn fares remained unaltered during the immediate post-war period. The currency reform in the western zones, and so in the western sectors of Berlin in June 1948, led to the first problems. Until April 1949, DR would not accept payment in DM for any rail fare and when this policy was changed in April 1949, they found that few West Berliners were prepared to part with hard currency for an S-Bahn journey. By this time the two currencies had begun to drift apart and the eastern Mark (M) was valued at about 20% of the DM. As a result, receipts, especially in the west, became seriously out of step with running costs. To remedy this situation, DR introduced a massive fare increase on 10 May 1949, with an extremely complicated tariff, so complicated in practice that queues of up to 700 were recorded at ticket offices! The next day, the war tariff was re-introduced. However, almost immediately afterwards, from 21 May to 30 June, S-Bahn employees in West Berlin went on strike demanding that their wages should be paid in DM and in this they were partially successful. When services resumed on 1 July, it was therefore essential for DR to maximise its income in DM and from that date, this became the only accepted currency at stations in West Berlin. To distinguish them, DM tickets were printed in red, as opposed to the usual black. This system penalised many of those who lived in the east and to allow them to return from western stations, return tickets were introduced. As many westerners took advantage of these, by starting their journey in the east, returns from stations in the west were also introduced from October of the same year. Ten-day tickets (Dekadenkarten) were introduced in the west on 20 July 1949 and in the east on 20 January 1950.

Workers' tickets were introduced on 27 May 1952, but only for those whose place of work lay in East Berlin or the DDR. The price of these tickets was based on distance, not on the zone system. Transfer tickets to the system of BVG-Ost were reintroduced for price-level '1' on 17 May 1954 and were extended to level '2' on 1 March 1955. Arguments about insurance and responsibility in the event of an accident prevented their extension to BVG-West. With the increasing political tension and the building of the Outer Ring, certain groups of people living in East Berlin or the DDR were obliged to use it for all journeys and forbidden to travel through West Berlin. As a consequence of this, the S-Bahn tariff was extended to many other lines between 1950 and 1961. For journeys over the Outer Ring, fares were, until 1962, calculated on the same basis as if the journey had been made through West Berlin.

The closure of the frontier in August 1961 did not at first have any great effect on fares in the east and it was not until 1 December 1962 that alterations were made to take account of the new situation. In the meantime, S-Bahn season tickets were recognised on certain lines of BVG-Ost. The main change made in 1962 was the introduction of combined BVG-Ost/S-Bahn weekly tickets and the extension of transfer single tickets to price levels '3' and '4'. As the ring system, viewed from the east, now had a large hole in it, it no longer formed a logical basis for the fare structure, and so the areas lying to the west of West Berlin were redesignated Area price levels (Bereichspreisstufen). There were in all six of these and they were treated as the equivalent of the former ring zones, each forming one zone for the calculation of fare levels. While this led to increases for certain longer journeys, local fares in the new areas were generally reduced.

Thereafter, few changes were made in East Berlin. When BVG-Ost went over to one-person operation on buses and trams, transfer tickets were abolished and in their place five-journey tickets and monthly tickets were issued, valid on both systems. As the building of the Wall had reduced the demand for return tickets, these were withdrawn in 1966/67. Tourist day tickets were introduced on 1 July 1970, for both the S-Bahn alone (1M) and for combined S-Bahn/BVB services (2M). Like any ticket which was not cancelled at the beginning of the journey, these had to be held up for inspection by other passengers when entering a station, a habit which some visitors from the west found hard to remember and even harder to practice! As more and more machines came into use, it became possible to use several tickets at a lower fare to make up the fare for a longer journey – machines issued tickets for price levels 1 to 3 only. From 1 February 1976, common tickets were issued for price level '1' and single journeys on BVB vehicles.

The opening of the extension of U-Bahn line 5 on 1 July 1989 allowed for the first time cross-platform interchange between U-Bahn and S-Bahn (at Wuhletal) and to take account of this, transfer tickets were reintroduced, valid only for these systems and not on trams or buses. This was the last change made by DR before the opening of the frontier in November 1989. In few other cities was the basic single fare (20 Pf) still that of 1944!

Rather surprisingly, the building of the Wall had no effect on the fare system of the S-Bahn in West Berlin for several years. It was not until 1 July 1966 that changes were made, in that price level '2' became the minimum for journeys both within West Berlin and to stations in the east. This represented a disguised fare increase of 50% for many passengers. At the same time the Dekadenkarten were replaced by weekly tickets and all seasons were valid for the entire western system. There were further increases between 1972 and 1983, although DR always maintained the basic single fare at a level below that current on BVG. A tourist ticket (two days) was also introduced in the west. From 1 November 1979 fares to stations in the east were also increased, as these were now calculated by adding the fare to Friedrichstrasse to that from that station to destination, and for these journeys a new price level '9' was created – later there was also a level '10'. Finally on 1 August 1981, the zone system within West Berlin was abandoned in favour of a new price level 'S', thus breaking the last link with the war tariff. By 1983, the single fare in West Berlin was DM 2.

After the takeover of the S-Bahn in West Berlin by the Senate, fares were aligned with those of the BVG and tickets were inter-available on all forms of transport.

The first effect of the changes was the introduction, on 1 January 1990, of tickets sold in the east for 2 M (two hours validity) or 5 M (24 hours), which were valid on all forms of transport in both the west and the east, and also in Potsdam. This facility allowed DDR citizens to buy tickets available in the west with their own currency, BVG having withdrawn the previous concession which allowed them free travel in the west – in practice, almost all DDR visitors had been senior citizens. For the first time also, BVG tickets were recognised in the east. With the currency union of 1 July 1990, all tickets were priced in DM.

It was not until 1 August 1991 that a new tariff structure was introduced, when the eight price levels were abolished and in their place a flat fare of DM 1.80 was introduced, with a short-distance (three stations) tickets available for 70 Pf. At the same time, a common tariff was instituted for BVG, BVB, DR S-Bahn, Potsdam Transport and the three suburban tramway undertakings in the east. All tickets were now to BVG design, although those for the eastern S-Bahn continued to carry the DR emblem. By 1995 the basic ticket had reached the price of DM 3.70 and the short-distance ticket DM 2.50, but the availability of four-journey tickets and other facilities such as the "Environment Ticket" (Umweltkarte) somewhat mitigated the extent of the increase over 1991 fare levels.

Also available are 30-hour tickets (DM 15.00 for one person, DM 20.00 for two persons), three-day tickets (Welcome card for DM 29.00) and a seven-day ticket for DM 40.00. Every ticket has to be validated before the start of the first journey, either by personnel or by machines.

Appendix One: Rolling Stock Preserved

Historische S-Bahn e.v. – the S-Bahn Museum Group

When in the late 1980s the last examples of certain types of S-Bahn rolling stock began to disappear, either through scrapping or modernisation, it became clear that if a representative selection were to be kept, private individuals would have to supplement the official effort. In October 1991, therefore, the association Historische S-Bahn e.V. was founded, the aim being to preserve as many as possible of the historic trains and to run special trips with at least some of them. The group began with a membership of 27, which in its first four years grew to over 400. Members come from a wide range of occupations and now include some enthusiasts from overseas. Membership is divided into two categories, active and supporting. Members in the former category must spend at least 50 hours per year working on these trains or on associated tasks.

Since its foundation the association has succeeded in preserving 17 S-Bahn vehicles and naturally the main efforts have been concentrated on bringing these into secure covered storage. After spending some time in a variety of locations around Berlin, most of the vehicles have now been brought together at Hundekehle sheds at Grunewald. The collection is not at present open to the public.

The collection consists of the following:

1. Class ET/EB169 "Bernau" (1925)
   The front portion of an unrebuilt motor coach of this type, ET169.005b, was located in Schöneweide workshops and has now been brought into the Museum collection. It had been withdrawn in 1943 and was used as a store, still showing traces of its wartime condition. There are also two of the four-wheel trailers in the collection, EB169.006b and 169.015a.

2. Class ET/EB168 "Oranienburg" (1926)
   A motor and former control trailer have been preserved, ET168.029 and EB168.030 respectively. The latter has been used as a luggage van and will need considerable work to the bogies to restore it to running order.

3. Class ET/EB165.8 (later 275.9 & 475) "Wannseebahn" (1932)
   A motor and a trailer have been earmarked for preservation by the group (275.959 and 275.966) but at the moment they both form part of the reserve stock of S-Bahn Berlin. The motor car is a prototype vehicle in having rectangular cab windows instead of the standard upward sloping cab windows.

4. Class ET/EB125 and 166 (later 276, 477 & 877) "Bankier/Olympiazug" (1934)
   From the prototype train of these classes, the group has acquired a quarter train, consisting of motor and trailer – set 276.031 and 276.032.

5. Class ET/EB167 (later 166, 276.0, 277 & 477) "1938/41" class (1938–41)
   Historische S-Bahn e.V. has been fortunate to acquire the last two non-modernised two-car trains from this class – 277.003/004 and 277.087/088.

6. Class ET/ES167 (later 166, 276.0, 277 & 477) "Peenemünde" class (1941)
   A two-car train has been preserved, consisting of cars 276.069/070. It will require a good deal of work to make it suitable for operation.

7. Class 270 (later 485/885) Prototype (1979)
   One of the two-car sets from the class 270 prototype train has been preserved comprising 270.001/002.

Part of a section of a 'Bernau' class motor coach of 1925 has been rescued for preservation from Schöneweide workshops by the S-Bahn Museum Group. The surviving vehicle is seen in the depot yard at Hundekehle. *Brian Hardy*

Other vehicles owned by the group include the following:

ET169.017a ⎫	ex 278.005–008
ET169.017b ⎪	
EB169.006c ⎬	
EB169.017b ⎭	
ET165.040 ⎫	as 275.625/626
EB165.040 ⎭	
ET165.825	as 475.126
EB165.815	as 875.125

It can thus be seen that the Museum Group has successfully saved at least one example of each type of train which has to date been withdrawn. Much work remains to be done and additional support is always welcome. Enquiries about membership should be addressed to:

Historische S-Bahn e.V.
Wönnichstrasse 21
10317 Berlin
Tel (from UK): 00 49 30 297 17474
Fax (from UK): 00 49 30 336 8260

Note that the above is for postal and telephone enquiries only.

A souvenir stand is open on the platform of Köpenick S-Bahn station (line S3) every Thursday evening between 17.00 and 20.00.

S-Bahn GmbH – The "Traditionzug" of S-Bahn Berlin:

As far back as 1984, DR began to consider the possibility of restoring a set of Stadtbahn class to its original condition and using it for special tours. The set selected consisted of class 275.659/660 which, in time for the city's 750th anniversary celebrations in 1987, reappeared in service as Nos. 2303 and 5447. The train has been beautifully restored and includes a second class area again – this may be distinguished by the blue window surround. Since then a further three two-car sets have been preserved and special trips are frequently run with these, being often crewed by members of the Historische S-Bahn who are professional railway staff. They also appear at open days or special events, such as the reopening of closed sections of line. Information about such outings may be obtained about two weeks in advance by telephoning 00 49 30 463 9365.

Cars preserved are:

ET165.155 ex–2303	ET165.231	ET165.471	ET165.555 ex–3662
ES165.155 ex–5446	ES165.231	EB165.471	EB165.555 ex–6121

Verkehrsmuseum Nürnberg:

ET165.334 ex–3412
EB165.334 ex–6301

Berlin Museum für Verkehr und Technik:

ET165.338 ex–275.747
ES165.338 ex–275.748
ET125.001 ex–276.035

In Use as Cafés:

ET166.059 ex–276.075 }	Falkensee, Seegefelder Strasse, junction
ES166.059 ex–276.076 ∫	Dortmunder Strasse
EB167.021 ex–277.028	Hennigsdorf, Spandauer Allee/Klara-Schabbel Strasse/Trappenallee

In Private Ownership:

ET165.484 ex–275.529	Beerfelden-Gammelsbach, Odenwald.

Reserved in July 1995 for possible use as 'garden sheds' in the Falkensee/Albrechtshof area:

475.021	475.077
875.021	875.077

Appendix Two: Current Rolling Stock List

Apart from the modern classes of train (480 and 485), the rolling stock of the S-Bahn has been the subject of renumbering, the current series being the fifth to affect the oldest stock and implemented from 1 January 1992. The previous renumbering schemes took place in 1924, 1930, 1942 and 1970. It was then the practice to number motor coaches in 'odd' numbers, with trailers and control trailers given 'even' numbers. The latest scheme has seen the last three digits of pairs of cars numbered identically, with a different first three digit type number to distinguish motors from trailers and control trailers, beginning with '4' and '8' respectively. This has been applied to the new class 485 stock, but with the class 480 cars, which are all driving motors, the second motor car in the pair has been numbered '500' upwards.

All S-Bahn passenger vehicles, however, are numbered to the UIC standard, having seven numbers. Apart from the class (first three numbers), and the vehicle number (second three digits), there is also a seventh 'check' digit, which is calculated by a complex formula by computer. This seventh number is provided to verify the integrity of the six main numbers.

Trains are allocated to the following depots for maintenance purposes:

GA	Grünau
FF	Friedrichfelde
WS	Wannsee

Class 475 Stock

DMSO		TSO	DMSO		TSO	DMSO		TSO	DMSO		DTSO
475.003	WS	875.003	†475.042	WS	875.042	†475.084	WS	875.084	475.601	FF	875.601
†475.004	WS	875.004	475.043	WS	875.043	*475.086	WS	875.086	475.602	FF	875.602
475.005	WS	875.005	475.044	WS	875.044	475.091	WS	875.091	475.603	FF	875.603
†475.007	WS	875.007	475.049	WS	875.049	*475.092	WS	875.092	475.604	FF	875.604
475.009	WS	875.009	475.051	WS	875.051	475.094	WS	875.094	475.605	FF	875.605
475.011	WS	875.011	475.052	WS	875.052	*475.098	WS	875.098	475.606	FF	875.606
475.017	WS	875.017	475.054	WS	875.054	475.099	WS	875.099	475.607	FF	875.607
†475.019	WS	875.019	475.057	WS	875.057	*475.100	WS	875.100	475.608	FF	875.608
475.024	WS	875.024	†475.058	WS	875.058	475.101	WS	875.101	475.609	FF	875.609
475.025	WS	875.025	*475.060	WS	875.060	*475.102	WS	875.102	475.610	FF	875.610
475.028	WS	875.028	475.065	WS	875.065	475.103	WS	875.103	475.611	FF	875.611
†475.030	WS	875.030	*475.070	WS	875.070	*475.104	FF	875.104	475.612	FF	875.612
475.031	WS	875.031	475.073	WS	875.073	*475.108	FF	875.108	475.613	FF	875.613
475.032	WS	875.032	*475.074	WS	875.074	*475.110	FF	875.110	475.614	FF	875.614
475.033	WS	875.033	475.075	WS	875.075	*475.111	FF	875.111	475.615	FF	875.615
475.034	WS	875.034	475.076	WS	875.076	*475.114	FF	875.114			
475.037	WS	875.037	475.078	WS	875.078	*475.122	FF	875.122			
475.039	WS	875.039	475.079	WS	875.079	*475.123	FF	875.123			
475.040	WS	875.040	475.080	WS	875.080	*475.124	FF	875.124			

All sets ex-BVG except those marked * ex-DR

†Unit without train radio.

Class 476 Stock

DMSO		TSO	DMSO		TSO	DMSO		TSO	DMSO		TSO
476.001	FF	876.001	476.046	FF	876.046	476.313	FF	876.313	476.363	FF	876.363
476.002	FF	876.002	476.047	FF	876.047	476.314	FF	876.314	476.364	WS	876.364
476.003	FF	876.003	476.048	FF	876.048	476.316	FF	876.316	476.365	FF	876.365
476.004	FF	876.004	476.049	FF	876.049	476.317	FF	876.317	476.366	WS	876.366
476.005	FF	876.005	476.050	FF	876.050	476.318	FF	876.318	476.367	FF	876.367
476.006	FF	876.006	476.051	FF	876.051	476.319	FF	876.319	476.369	FF	876.369
476.007	FF	876.007	476.052	FF	876.052	476.320	FF	876.320	476.371	FF	876.371
476.008	FF	876.008	476.053	FF	876.053	476.321	FF	876.321	476.372	FF	876.372
476.009	FF	876.009	476.054	FF	876.054	476.322	FF	876.322	476.373	FF	876.373
476.010	FF	876.010	476.055	FF	876.055	476.323	FF	876.323	476.374	FF	876.374
476.011	FF	876.011	476.056	FF	876.056	476.324	FF	876.324	476.375	FF	876.375
476.012	FF	876.012	476.057	FF	876.057	476.325	FF	876.325	476.378	FF	876.378
476.013	FF	876.013	476.058	FF	876.058	476.326	FF	876.326	476.379	FF	876.379
476.014	FF	876.014	476.059	FF	876.059	476.327	FF	876.327	476.380	FF	876.380
476.015	FF	876.015	476.060	FF	876.060	476.328	FF	876.328	476.381	FF	876.381
476.016	FF	876.016	476.061	FF	876.061	476.329	FF	876.329	476.382	FF	876.382
476.017	FF	876.017	476.062	FF	876.062	476.330	FF	876.330	476.383	WS	876.383
476.018	FF	876.018	476.063	FF	876.063	476.331	FF	876.331	476.384	FF	876.384
476.019	FF	876.019	476.064	FF	876.064	476.332	FF	876.332	476.385	WS	876.385
476.020	FF	876.020	476.065	FF	876.065	476.333	FF	876.333	476.386	FF	876.386
476.021	FF	876.021	476.066	FF	876.066	476.334	WS	876.334	476.387	FF	876.387
476.022	FF	876.022	476.067	FF	876.067	476.335	FF	876.335	476.388	FF	876.388
476.023	FF	876.023	476.068	FF	876.068	476.336	FF	876.336	476.389	FF	876.389
476.024	FF	876.024	476.069	FF	876.069	476.337	FF	876.337	476.390	FF	876.390
476.025	FF	876.025	476.070	FF	876.070	476.338	FF	876.338	476.391	FF	876.391
476.026	FF	876.026	476.071	FF	876.071	476.339	FF	876.339	476.392	FF	876.392
476.027	FF	876.027	476.072	FF	876.072	476.341	FF	876.341	476.393	FF	876.393
476.028	FF	876.028	476.073	FF	876.073	476.342	FF	876.342	476.394	FF	876.394
476.029	FF	876.029	476.074	FF	876.074	476.345	FF	876.345	476.395	FF	876.395
476.030	FF	876.030	476.075	FF	876.075	476.346	WS	876.346	476.396	FF	876.396
476.031	FF	876.031	476.076	FF	876.076	476.347	FF	876.347	476.397	FF	876.397
476.032	FF	876.032	476.077	FF	876.077	476.348	FF	876.348	476.398	FF	876.398
476.033	FF	876.033	476.078	FF	876.078	476.349	FF	876.349	476.399	FF	876.399
476.034	FF	876.034	476.079	FF	876.079	476.350	FF	876.350	476.400	FF	876.400
476.035	FF	876.035	476.301	FF	876.301	476.351	FF.	876.351	476.401	FF	876.401
476.036	FF	876.036	476.302	FF	876.302	476.352	FF	876.352	476.402	FF	876.402
476.037	FF	876.037	476.303	FF	876.303	476.353	FF	876.353	476.403	FF	876.403
476.038	FF	876.038	476.304	FF	876.304	476.354	FF	876.354	476.404	FF	876.404
476.039	FF	876.039	476.305	FF	876.305	476.355	FF	876.355	476.405	FF	876.405
476.040	FF	876.040	476.306	FF	876.306	476.356	FF	876.356	476.406	WS	876.406
476.041	FF	876.041	476.307	FF	876.307	476.357	FF	876.357	476.407	WS	876.407
476.042	FF	876.042	476.309	FF	876.309	476.358	FF	876.358	476.408	FF	876.408
476.043	FF	876.043	476.310	FF	876.310	476.359	FF	876.359	476.409	FF	876.409
476.044	FF	876.044	476.311	FF	876.311	476.361	FF	876.361	476.410	FF	876.410
476.045	FF	876.045	476.312	FF	876.312	476.362	FF	876.362	476.411	FF	876.411

DMSO		TSO	DMSO		TSO	DMSO		TSO	DMSO		TSO
476.412	WS	876.412	476.420	WS	876.420	476.429	WS	876.429	476.447	FF	876.447
476.413	FF	876.413	476.421	FF	876.421	476.430	WS	876.430	476.459	FF	876.459
476.414	FF	876.414	476.422	FF	876.422	476.431	FF	876.431	476.460	FF	876.460
476.415	FF	876.415	476.423	FF	876.423	476.432	WS	876.432	476.461	WS	876.461
476.416	WS	876.416	476.424	WS	876.424	476.433	FF	876.433	476.462	WS	876.462
476.417	FF	876.417	476.425	FF	876.425	476.445	FF	876.445	476.463	FF	876.463
476.418	WS	876.418	476.427	WS	876.427	476.446	FF	876.446	476.470	FF	876.470
476.419	WS	876.419	476.428	WS	876.428						

Sets 476.001–876.001 to 476.079–876.079 are fitted with Knorr standard brakes.

Class 477 Stock

DMSO		TSO	DMSO		TSO	DMSO		TSO	DMSO		TSO
477.001	GA	877.001	477.034	GA	877.034	477.067	GA	877.067	477.100	GA	877.100
477.002	GA	877.002	477.035	GA	877.035	477.068	GA	877.068	477.101	GA	877.101
477.003	GA	877.003	477.036	GA	877.036	477.069	GA	877.069	477.102	GA	877.102
477.004	GA	877.004	477.037	GA	877.037	477.070	GA	877.070	477.103	GA	877.103
477.005	GA	877.005	477.038	GA	877.038	477.071	GA	877.071	477.104	GA	877.104
477.006	GA	877.006	477.039	GA	877.039	477.072	GA	877.072	477.105	GA	877.105
477.007	GA	877.007	477.040	GA	877.040	477.073	GA	877.073	477.106	GA	877.106
477.008	GA	877.008	*477.041	GA	*877.041	477.074	GA	877.074	477.107	GA	877.107
477.009	GA	877.009	477.042	GA	877.042	477.075	GA	877.075	477.108	GA	877.108
477.010	GA	877.010	477.043	GA	877.043	477.076	GA	877.076	477.109	GA	877.109
477.011	GA	877.011	477.044	GA	877.044	477.077	GA	877.077	477.110	GA	877.110
477.012	GA	877.012	477.045	GA	877.045	477.078	GA	877.078	477.111	GA	877.111
477.013	GA	877.013	477.046	GA	877.046	477.079	GA	877.079	477.112	GA	877.112
477.014	GA	877.014	477.047	GA	877.047	477.080	GA	877.080	477.113	GA	877.113
477.015	GA	877.015	477.048	GA	877.048	477.081	GA	877.081	477.114	GA	877.114
477.016	GA	877.016	477.049	GA	877.049	477.082	GA	877.082	477.115	GA	877.115
477.017	GA	877.017	477.050	GA	877.050	477.083	GA	877.083	477.116	GA	877.116
477.018	GA	877.018	477.051	GA	877.051	477.084	GA	877.084	477.117	GA	877.117
477.019	GA	877.019	477.052	GA	877.052	477.085	GA	877.085	477.118	GA	877.118
477.020	GA	877.020	477.053	GA	877.053	477.086	GA	877.086	477.119	GA	877.119
477.021	GA	877.021	477.054	GA	877.054	477.087	GA	877.087	477.120	GA	877.120
477.022	GA	877.022	477.055	GA	877.055	477.088	GA	877.088	477.121	GA	877.121
477.023	GA	877.023	477.056	GA	877.056	477.089	GA	877.089	477.122	GA	877.122
477.024	GA	877.024	477.057	GA	877.057	477.090	GA	877.090	477.123	GA	877.123
477.025	GA	877.025	477.058	GA	877.058	477.091	GA	877.091	477.124	FF	877.124
477.026	GA	877.026	477.059	GA	877.059	477.092	GA	877.092	477.125	FF	877.125
477.027	GA	877.027	477.060	GA	877.060	477.093	WS	877.093	477.126	FF	877.126
477.028	GA	877.028	477.061	GA	877.061	477.094	WS	877.094	477.127	FF	877.127
477.029	GA	877.029	477.062	GA	877.062	477.095	GA	877.095	477.128	FF	877.128
477.030	GA	877.030	477.063	GA	877.063	477.096	GA	877.096	477.129	FF	877.129
477.031	GA	877.031	477.064	GA	877.064	477.097	GA	877.097	477.130	FF	877.130
477.032	GA	877.032	477.065	GA	877.065	477.098	GA	877.098	477.131	FF	877.131
477.033	GA	877.033	477.066	GA	877.066	477.099	GA	877.099	477.132	FF	877.132

DMSO		TSO	DMSO		TSO	DMSO		TSO	DMSO		TSO
477.133	FF	877.133	477.152	FF	877.152	477.171	FF	877.171	477.190	FF	877.190
477.134	FF	877.134	477.153	FF	877.153	477.172	FF	877.172	477.191	FF	877.191
477.135	FF	877.135	477.154	FF	877.154	477.173	FF	877.173	477.192	FF	877.192
477.136	FF	877.136	477.155	FF	877.155	477.174	FF	877.174	477.193	FF	877.193
477.137	FF	877.137	477.156	FF	877.156	477.175	FF	877.175	477.194	FF	877.194
477.138	FF	877.138	477.157	FF	877.157	477.176	FF	877.176	477.195	FF	877.195
477.139	FF	877.139	477.158	FF	877.158	477.177	FF	877.177	477.196	FF	877.196
477.140	FF	877.140	477.159	FF	877.159	477.178	FF	877.178			
*477.141	GA	*877.141	477.160	FF	877.160	477.179	FF	877.179			
477.142	FF	877.142	477.161	FF	877.161	477.180	FF	877.180			
477.143	FF	877.143	477.162	FF	877.162	477.181	FF	877.181	DMSO		DTSO
477.144	FF	877.144	477.163	FF	877.163	477.182	FF	877.182	477.601	FF	877.601
477.145	FF	877.145	477.164	FF	877.164	477.183	FF	877.183	477.602	FF	877.602
477.146	FF	877.146	477.165	FF	877.165	477.184	FF	877.184	477.603	FF	877.603
477.147	FF	877.147	477.166	FF	877.166	477.185	FF	877.185	477.604	FF	877.604
477.148	FF	877.148	477.167	FF	877.167	477.186	FF	877.186	477.605	FF	877.605
477.149	FF	877.149	477.168	FF	877.168	477.187	FF	877.187	477.606	FF	877.606
477.150	FF	877.150	477.169	FF	877.169	477.188	FF	877.188	477.607	FF	877.607
477.151	FF	877.151	477.170	FF	877.170	477.189	FF	877.189	477.608	FF	877.608

Note * Units in all-over advertisement livery.

Class 480 Stock – all allocated to "WS"

DMSO	DMSO	DMSO	DMSO	DMSO	DMSO	DMSO	DMSO
BVG Prototypes:		480.021	480.521	480.044	480.544	480.065	480.565
480.001	480.501	480.022	480.522	480.045	480.545	480.066	480.566
480.002	480.502	480.023	480.523	Ex-DR Units:		480.067	480.567
480.003	480.503	480.024	480.524	480.046	480.546	480.068	480.568
480.004	480.504	480.026	480.526	480.047	480.547	480.069	480.569
Ex-BVG Units:		480.027	480.527	480.048	480.548	480.070	480.570
480.005	480.505	480.028	480.528	480.049	480.549	480.071	480.571
480.006	480.506	480.029	480.529	480.050	480.550	480.072	480.572
480.007	480.507	480.030	480.530	480.051	480.551	480.073	480.573
480.008	480.508	480.031	480.531	480.052	480.552	480.074	480.574
480.009	480.509	480.032	480.532	480.053	480.553	480.075	480.575
480.010	480.510	480.033	480.533	480.054	480.554	480.076	480.576
480.011	480.511	480.034	480.534	480.055	480.555	480.077	480.577
480.012	480.512	480.035	480.535	480.056	480.556	480.078	480.578
480.013	480.513	480.036	480.536	480.057	480.557	480.079	480.579
480.014	480.514	480.037	480.537	480.058	480.558	480.080	480.580
480.015	480.515	480.038	480.538	480.059	480.559	480.081	480.581
480.016	480.516	480.039	480.539	480.060	480.560	480.082	480.582
480.017	480.517	480.040	480.540	480.061	480.561	480.083	480.583
480.018	480.518	480.041	480.541	480.062	480.562	480.084	480.584
480.019	480.519	480.042	480.542	480.063	480.563	480.085	480.585
480.020	480.520	480.043	480.543	480.064	480.564		

Class 485 Stock

DMSO		TSO	DMSO		TSO	DMSO		TSO	DMSO		TSO
485.005	GA	885.005	485.049	GA	885.049	485.093	GA	885.093	485.137	GA	885.137
485.006	GA	885.006	485.050	GA	885.050	485.094	GA	885.094	485.138	GA	885.138
485.007	GA	885.007	485.051	GA	885.051	485.095	GA	885.095	485.139	GA	885.139
485.008	GA	885.008	485.052	GA	885.052	485.096	GA	885.096	485.140	GA	885.140
485.009	GA	885.009	485.053	GA	885.053	485.097	GA	885.097	485.141	GA	885.141
485.010	GA	885.010	485.054	GA	885.054	485.098	GA	885.098	485.142	GA	885.142
485.011	GA	885.011	485.055	GA	885.055	485.099	GA	885.099	485.143	GA	885.143
485.012	GA	885.012	485.056	GA	885.056	485.100	GA	885.100	485.144	GA	885.144
485.013	GA	885.013	485.057	GA	885.057	485.101	GA	885.101	485.145	GA	885.145
485.014	GA	885.014	485.058	GA	885.058	485.102	GA	885.102	485.146	GA	885.146
485.015	GA	885.015	485.059	GA	885.059	485.103	GA	885.103	485.147	GA	885.147
485.016	GA	885.016	485.060	GA	885.060	485.104	GA	885.104	485.148	GA	885.148
485.017	GA	885.017	485.061	GA	885.061	485.105	GA	885.105	485.149	GA	885.149
485.018	GA	885.018	485.062	GA	885.062	485.106	GA	885.106	485.150	GA	885.150
485.019	GA	885.019	485.063	GA	885.063	485.107	GA	885.107	485.151	GA	885.151
485.020	GA	885.020	485.064	GA	885.064	485.108	GA	885.108	485.152	GA	885.152
485.021	GA	885.021	485.065	GA	885.065	485.109	GA	885.109	485.153	GA	885.153
485.022	GA	885.022	485.066	GA	885.066	485.110	GA	885.110	485.154	GA	885.154
485.023	GA	885.023	485.067	GA	885.067	485.111	GA	885.111	485.155	GA	885.155
485.024	GA	885.024	485.068	GA	885.068	485.112	GA	885.112	485.156	GA	885.156
485.025	GA	885.025	485.069	GA	885.069	485.113	GA	885.113	485.157	GA	885.157
485.026	GA	885.026	485.070	GA	885.070	†485.114	FF	†885.114	485.158	GA	885.158
485.027	GA	885.027	485.071	GA	885.071	†485.115	FF	†885.115	485.159	GA	885.159
485.028	GA	885.028	485.072	GA	885.072	485.116	GA	885.116	485.160	GA	885.160
485.029	GA	885.029	485.073	GA	885.073	485.117	GA	885.117	485.161	GA	885.161
485.030	GA	885.030	485.074	GA	885.074	485.118	GA	885.118	485.162	GA	885.162
485.031	GA	885.031	485.075	GA	885.075	485.119	GA	885.119	485.163	GA	885.163
485.032	GA	885.032	485.076	GA	885.076	485.120	GA	885.120	485.164	GA	885.164
485.033	GA	885.033	485.077	GA	885.077	485.121	GA	885.121	485.165	GA	885.165
485.034	GA	885.034	485.078	GA	885.078	485.122	GA	885.122	485.166	GA	885.166
485.035	GA	885.035	485.079	GA	885.079	485.123	GA	885.123	485.167	GA	885.167
485.036	GA	885.036	485.080	GA	885.080	485.124	GA	885.124	485.168	GA	885.168
485.037	GA	885.037	485.081	GA	885.081	485.125	GA	885.125	485.169	GA	885.169
485.038	GA	885.038	485.082	GA	885.082	485.126	GA	885.126	485.170	GA	885.170
485.039	GA	885.039	485.083	GA	885.083	485.127	GA	885.127			
485.040	GA	885.040	485.084	GA	885.084	485.128	GA	885.128			
485.041	GA	885.041	485.085	GA	885.085	485.129	GA	885.129			
485.042	GA	885.042	485.086	GA	885.086	485.130	GA	885.130			
485.043	GA	885.043	485.087	GA	885.087	485.131	GA	885.131			
485.044	GA	885.044	485.088	GA	885.088	485.132	GA	885.132			
485.045	GA	885.045	485.089	GA	885.089	485.133	GA	885.133			
485.046	GA	885.046	485.090	GA	885.090	485.134	GA	885.134			
485.047	GA	885.047	485.091	GA	885.091	485.135	GA	885.135			
485.048	GA	885.048	485.092	GA	885.092	485.136	GA	885.136			

Note   † Duo-S-Bahn units, now out of service.

Class 481/482 Stock

DMSO	NDMC	Built by	DMSO	NDMC	Built by
481.001	482.001	DWA	481.006	482.006	AEG
481.002	482.002	AEG	481.007	482.007	DWA
481.003	482.003	DWA	481.008	482.008	AEG
481.004	482.004	AEG	481.009	482.009	DWA
481.005	482.005	DWA	481.010	482.010	DWA

DMSO   Driving motor second open
NDMC   Non-driving motor composite

Class 478 Internal Working Trains – ex-Passenger Stock

*478.004	878.004	FF	Breakdown Train Unit
*478.005	878.005	FF	Breakdown Train Unit
*478.006	878.006	FF	Stores Train Unit
*478.007	878.007	FF	Stores Train Unit
478.008			Tractor Unit (Schöneweide) named "Jumbo"
*478.014		FF	Ex-materials train, now used as storeroom
478.021		WS	Breakdown train
478.521		WS	Breakdown train
478.022		FF	Breakdown train
478.522		FF	Breakdown train

* Out of use

Summary of Passenger Stock:

TYPE	DMSO	DTSO	TSO	TOTAL
Class 475	72	15	57	144
Class 476	210	-	210	420
Class 477	204	8	196	408
Class 480	168	-	-	168
Class 485	166	-	166	332
TOTAL:	**820**	**23**	**629**	**1472**

Bibliography

Periodicals

Berliner Verkehrsblätter – from 1984 to date.

Der Stadtverkehr – from 1979 to date.

VB Kompress (Modelleisenbahn-Verband der DDR) – Nos. 1, 2 & 3.

Books

Berlin, the Biography of a City – A. Read and D. Fisher, Hutchinson, London, 1994.

The Fall of Berlin – A. Read and D. Fisher, Hutchinson, 1992.

Berliner S-Bahn – P. Bley, Alba 1993.

125 Jahre Strassenbahnen in Berlin – S. Hilkenbach and W. Kramer, Alba 1990.

Berliner Omnibusse – D. Gammrath, Alba 1988.

Geisterbahnhöfe – Westlinien unter Ostberlin – H. Knobloch, Ch. Links Verlag, Berlin 1992.

Die Flutung des Berliner S-Bahn Tunnels – Rekonstruktion und Legenden – K. Meyer, Kunstamt Kreuzberg 1992.

S- und U-Bahn Architektur in Berlin – H-W Klünner, Senate of West Berlin, 1985.

Das Berliner U- und S-Bahnnetz, eine Geschichte in Streckenplänen – A. Gottwaldt, Argon, Berlin 1995.

Züge aus die Vergangenheit, Die Berliner S-Bahn – G. Armanski und W. Hebold-Heitz, Transit, Berlin 1981.

Berlin Baut – Nos. 14 & 16. Published by the Senate of Berlin, Building Department, 1993 and 1995. (These publications deal with the southern part of the Ring and the S-Bahn reopenings).

50 Jahre BVG, 1929–1979 – BVG 1979.

Typisch Berlin, ein BVG Portrait – BVG 1987.

Nord-Süd S-Bahn – Special number of Signal, Interessengemenschaft Eisenbahn und Nahverkehr Berlin 1992.

Strecke ohne Ende, Die Berliner Ringbahn – IGEB 1993.

S-Bahn nach Teltow – IGEB 1995.

Tramway & Light Railway Atlas, Germany 1992 – LRTA London, 1993.

German Railways, Locomotives & Multiple Units – Platform 5 Publications, Sheffield, 1993.

BVG and VEB(K)BVB – various timetables, maps and publicity leaflets.